# Simple
# Soulful
# Savory too

Healthy Family Recipes

IJABA Publishing Inc
PO Box 372425
Denver, CO 8237

ISBN 13: 978-0-9847316-9-5
ISBN 10: 0-9847316-9-5

Library of Congress
Cataloging-in-Publication Data

**Editors**
Jane Brunton
Laura Anderson
Patricia M. Duncan

**Creative Director/Designer**
Jane Brunton

**Photographer**
*Photograph of author (back cover), Yeast Rolls (p. 23) and Mixed Greens (p. 102)*
Sam Pegues

To purchase this book in bulk, email ijabapublish@gmail.com
to place your order.

# Foreword

When Jo Ann asked me to write this foreword, I thought, doesn't she really want somebody famous to help boost the sales of her book? Then I realized—she doesn't need a celebrity endorsement. Jo Ann is already a bit of a celebrity herself. After all, the first edition of this book was a best seller, and she has personally touched so many people with her gift of cooking and nutrition expertise.

However, we have been friends for 40 years so I can certainly tell you a couple of stories about why I admire Jo Ann. One that comes to mind is the story of our first office computer.

When we worked together at the U.S. Administration on Aging, our very first office computer was delivered and placed on a desk in the middle of our open space. None of us knew how to use it, and no one bothered to offer any training. That big beige box sat for days like a lonely albatross until Jo Ann finally jumped up and said, well, I'm going to find out what this is all about. And she was the first brave soul to tame the beast. That same fortitude and willingness to tackle new ideas and embrace innovation was steadfast throughout her career, and those qualities continue to be exemplified in this book.

Whether in a community group, a classroom, a senior program, or on a national stage at a conference, Jo Ann has always been committed to making a difference in people's lives and health. Throughout the years she has been a passionate and formidable advocate for some of the most vulnerable in our community. One of the things I admire most about Jo Ann is the dignity and respect with which she treats everyone she encounters.

Jo Ann's cooking skills are legendary, but this generosity in sharing her culinary knowledge and techniques with diverse audiences is what sets her apart. And no matter the setting, she never misses an opportunity to make the experiences fun and enjoyable. This book is yet another opportunity for Jo Ann to share her caring, her joy, and her passion for healthful, delicious meals.

*Sharon Larson*
*Littleton, CO*

---

*"Jo Ann Pegues' book is an irresistible invitation to share the foods from generations of not only her hearth, but also of her heart. Her tempting and beloved family recipes will become your family's favorite dishes too."*

*Mary Lee Chin, MS RDN*
*Nutrition Edge Communications*

# Introduction

The incentive for writing this cookbook came from requests for recipes I have prepared and shared over the years either in cooking classes, meals at home or for groups and organizations. We all remember favorite foods and meals prepared by family members that we never learned

*I don't consider myself a gourmet cook, however, I enjoy preparing and serving food to fill stomachs and warm hearts.*

to prepare. We all have recipes that have been saved over the years, recorded on cards and the backs of envelopes, church bulletins and other scraps of paper.

I don't consider myself a gourmet cook, however, I enjoy preparing and serving food to fill stomachs and warm hearts. My grandchildren often put a stamp of approval on the meals I prepare for them. I am often asked by my children and grandchildren how to prepare certain foods. Some of the foods I prepare, I learned by watching my mother. She did not always follow a recipe except when she made cakes or other desserts. Many of the recipes she just remembered. I have recreated some of these foods from memory, revising until I get the taste that I remember.

In this cookbook I attempt to capture my favorite recipes along with other family members' and friends' recipes, in order to preserve these established traditions.

Mealtime was a highlight in our home. We had three meals every day:

breakfast, dinner and supper. Meals always included foods that were grown or raised on our farm: meat, potatoes and vegetables. All meals were prepared and eaten at home because eating out was not an option in those years. Mother cooked large meals, usually on Saturday for Sunday dinner. In addition to having invited and uninvited guests for dinner, she packaged food to take to neighbors and friends who were ill and or unable to get out. We had our own home delivered meals long before that term became known in government programs and the volunteer community.

My dad, George Millsap, was born in 1889 and raised in Pontotoc County and New Albany, Mississippi. He left Mississippi as a young man in search of a better life and settled in Oklahoma. He began farming and over the years made a name for himself in agriculture. For example, he received accolades from Oklahoma A & M College for his farming techniques. He was a proud man, who worked hard to provide for his family.

My sister often shares stories about Dad, a true lover of meat and sweets. He wanted dessert with each meal. My mother always had 'tea cakes' so that there was always something sweet available. My sister recounts the story about the recipe for Mock Apple Pie on the Ritz Cracker box; mock because there were no apples in the pie. The recipe used crackers instead. My sister had eaten some Mock Apple Pie at a friend's home and was so excited that she told our parents about the pie and asked if we could have some. Our dad respond-

ed, "We have apples and if there is going to be pie, it will be with real apples, not crackers." He explained that maybe her friends didn't have any apples.

When I was growing up I was a 4-H club member. The values and skills I learned in 4-H have guided me throughout life. The pledge: "I pledge my head to clearer thinking, my heart to greater loyalty, my hands to larger service and my health to better living for my club, my community, my country and my world." As a Registered Dietitian/Nutritionist I continue to live this pledge.

My passion throughout my career has been to educate and help clients, family and friends to eat healthier and lower risks of nutrition related diseases and disorders (diabetes, heart disease, high blood pressure etc.) that disproportionately impact our population.

I have modified, tested and provided the nutritional analysis for several of the recipes to decrease salt, fat, and sugar, making them diabetic friendly, heart healthy and tasty. Vegetable recipes have been modified using seasonings other than meat to make them healthy. Ordinary vegetables are prepared in extraordinary ways. Other recipes are provided by family members who wanted to share their favorites. I hope you will try and enjoy them all.

Some of the diabetic friendly recipes were adapted from *The Soul Food Cookbook for people with Diabetes*.

**Jo Ann Millsap Pegues RDN, MPA**

# Dedication

*To my mother, Laurene Millsap, who always had food to serve anyone who graced our home and to my dad, George Millsap, who taught me to always do my best. To my grandchildren as a guide to eating healthy and to prepare simple, soulful, and savory meals.*

# Acknowledgements

*My family members and friends, who willingly shared their favorite recipes, thank you. Thanks to my husband, Sam, for his patience and encouragement; he has always been my rock in all my endeavors and to my children and grandchildren who always ask, "How is the cookbook coming?"*

# Table of Contents

# Appetizers

# SARDINE LOVERS' SNACK

*This is Sam's favorite especially with Ritz Crackers.*

## Ingredients

2 cans sardines (water packed)
1/4 cup sweet relish
1/3 cup mayonnaise
1/2 cup green olives, chopped
2 stalks celery, chopped
1/2 medium Vidalia onion, chopped
3 hard-boiled eggs, coarsely chopped

## Directions:

- Mix all ingredients together and serve with assorted crackers.
- Cover and keep refrigerated.

---

# SPINACH BALLS

*A great appetizer! This recipe was given to me years ago by a co-worker.*

## Ingredients

10 ounces frozen chopped spinach
1/2 cup chopped onion
2 eggs, beaten
1/3 cup butter, melted
1 cup stuffing mix, crushed (Pepperidge Farm®)
1/4 cup Parmesan cheese
1 clove garlic, minced
1/2 tsp thyme
1/2 tsp pepper

## Directions

- Cook and drain spinach.
- Mix spinach, onion, eggs, butter, cheese, garlic, thyme and pepper.
- Add stuffing crumbs and mix thoroughly.
- Shape into balls and chill for several hours to blend flavors.
- Bake in 350 degree oven for 15 minutes.

# LITTLE PIZZAS

*My niece, Semret, shared this recipe as a fun one to do with children.
Depending on age, they can help with preparation.*

## Ingredients

English muffins

tomato or pizza sauce

garlic powder

grated mozzarella cheese

small pepperoni slices

oregano

## Directions

- Preheat oven to 400 degrees.
- Spread sauce on muffin halves; add cheese, oregano, garlic powder and top with pepperoni.
- Bake for about 5 minutes.

# BLACK BEAN AND CORN SALAD

*Can be eaten as a side dish, salad or an appetizer with corn chips.*

## Ingredients

1/3 cup fresh lime juice

1/2 cup olive oil

1 clove garlic, minced

1 tsp salt

1/4 tsp ground cayenne pepper

2 (15 oz) cans black beans (no salt added) rinsed and drained

1 1/2 cups frozen corn kernels

1 large avocado, peeled, pitted and diced

1 red bell pepper, chopped

1 (15 oz) package grape tomatoes, halved

6 green onions, thinly sliced

1/2 cup fresh cilantro, chopped

## Directions

- Place lime juice, olive oil, garlic, salt, and cayenne pepper in a small jar. Cover with lid, and shake until ingredients are well mixed.
- In a salad bowl, combine beans, corn, avocado, bell pepper, tomatoes, green onions, and cilantro. Shake lime dressing, and pour it over the salad. Stir salad to coat vegetables and beans with dressing, and serve.

# JALAPENO CHEESE SQUARES

*My nephew, Kevin, shared this recipe.*

## Ingredients

- 4 cup cheddar cheese, grated
- 4 eggs, beaten
- 1 tsp onion, minced
- 4 Jalapeno peppers, seeded and chopped

## Directions

- Preheat oven to 350 degrees.
- Combine all ingredients and mix well.
- Spread into an ungreased 8-inch square pan.
- Bake for 30 minutes.
- Cut into 1-inch squares.

# Notes

# Breads

*During my 4-H Club years, I learned to present food demonstrations to an audience. My individual specialty was yeast rolls (see page 22). The process I used was to bake some rolls in advance for my display, and then I would mix a batch that would be rising while I demonstrated to the audience how to mix and knead the dough. Kneading the dough until it was smooth and elastic with air bubbles under the surface resulted in an ideal product. My home demonstration agent encouraged me along the way in 4-H club. She would identify venues where I could provide rolls and practice my craft. The skills I acquired while doing food demonstrations are values utilized in my volunteer activities with groups and organizations today.*

# BRAN MUFFINS

## Ingredients

1 3/4 cups all-purpose or whole wheat flour

1/2 cup sugar or Splenda®

3/4 tsp soda

3/4 tsp baking powder

1 cup buttermilk

1 egg or 1/2 cup egg substitute

1/4 cup salad oil

1 Tbsp orange juice

3/4 tsp grated orange rind

1 cup bran cereal

1 cup dried cranberries or raisins

3/4 cup chopped walnuts

## Directions

- Preheat oven to 350 degrees
- Combine dry ingredients in large bowl. Make a well in center.
- Add milk, eggs, oil, egg, orange juice and rind to dry mixture and stir until just moistened.
- Fold in bran cereal, nuts and cranberries.
- Spoon batter into prepared muffin cups.
- Bake 350 degrees for 15-20 minutes.

# CORN BREAD DRESSING

## Ingredients

4 Tbsp reduced fat margarine

1 cup onion, chopped

3 cups celery, chopped

2 cloves garlic, crushed

1/4 cup parsley, chopped

2 slices whole wheat bread, dried

5 cups leftover cornbread

1 tsp thyme

1 tsp sage

1 tsp marjoram

1 tsp pepper

1/2 tsp salt

2 cups egg substitute

2 cups turkey broth

## Directions

- Preheat oven to 350 degrees.
- Heat margarine in a large skillet and sauté the onion, celery, garlic, and parsley for 10 minutes.
- Put whole-wheat bread and corn bread in a large bowl and crumble into small pieces.
- Add spices to bread and mix well.
- Add onion mixture and stir.
- Add egg substitute and mix well; add cool turkey broth and stir.
- Pour dressing into a nonstick baking pan and bake for 45 minutes.

Note: For variety, try adding chestnuts, mushrooms, olives or reduced-fat sausages to this dressing.

## Nutrition

Fat: 4g; Saturated Fat: 0 g; Cholesterol: 1 mg; Sodium: 585 mg; Carbohydrate: 30g; Fiber: 3g; Sugar: 5g; Protein: 13g

# CRANBERRY MUFFINS

Yield: 12 servings

## Ingredients

3/4 cup all-purpose flour

3/4 cup whole wheat flour

1/2 cup brown sugar packed

2 tsp baking powder

1 tsp cinnamon

1/2 tsp ginger

1/4 tsp salt

1/2 cup skim milk

1/4 oup vcgctable oil

1/4 cup unsweetened applesauce

1/2 cup dried cranberries

1/2 cup chopped pecans optional

## Directions

- Preheat oven to 350 degrees.
- Spray muffin cups with cooking spray.
- Combine all-purpose flour, whole wheat flour, brown sugar, baking powder, cinnamon, ginger and salt in bowl and mix well.
- Combine skim milk, oil and applesauce in a bowl and mix well.
- Add to flour mixture stirring just until moistened. Fold in cranberries and pecans; spoon into prepared muffin cups.
- Bake for 20 minutes.

## Nutrition

Calories 167 kcal; Protein: 2g; Carbohydrates: 26g; Fat: 7g; Fiber: 2g; Sodium: 139mg

# BAKED HUSH PUPPIES

## Ingredients

2/3 cup yellow corn meal

1/3 cup all-purpose flour

1 tsp baking powder

1/3 cup finely chopped onion

1/3 cup skim milk

1 Tbsp vegetable oil (canola or safflower)

1 Tbsp chopped parsley

1/8 tsp pepper

1 egg white, beaten, or egg substitute

vegetable oil cooking spray

## Directions

- Preheat oven to 450 degrees.
- Combine cornmeal, flour and baking powder in medium bowl; make a well in center of mixture.
- Combine onion, milk, vegetable oil, parsley, pepper and egg whites.
- Add to dry ingredients, stirring just until moistened.
- Spoon 1 Tbsp batter per hush puppy into miniature muffin pans coated with cooking spray.
- Bake for 10 minutes or until lightly browned; remove from pans immediately.

# SOUTHERN STYLE CORNBREAD

## Ingredients

3 Tbsp vegetable oil

1 1/2 cups yellow cornmeal, whole grain

1 1/2 cups whole wheat flour

1/3 cup powered nonfat milk

1 1/2 Tbsp baking powder

3 large egg whites

1 1/2 cups fat free milk

## Directions

- Preheat oven to 450 degrees.
- Pour 1 tablespoon of oil into 10 1/2 inch cast-iron skillet or into a 9 x 11-inch pan. Set aside.
- In a bowl, mix cornmeal, flour, powdered milk and baking powder; set aside.
- In another bowl, beat egg whites with a whisk until slightly frothy. Add milk and remaining oil and whisk again. Pour liquid ingredients into dry ingredients and mix, but do not over mix (some lumps will remain).
- Place skillet or dish in oven 3 or 4 minutes to heat the oil. Watch time carefully. Pour batter into hot skillet or dish. Bake 20 minutes. Immediately remove from pan by turning onto a cutting board.

# YEAST ROLLS

*This is the same recipe that I demonstrated years ago in 4-H Club.*

## Ingredients

1 cup skim free milk, scalded

1/2 cup butter or margarine

1/2 cup sugar

1 tsp salt

1 package dry yeast

1/4 cup tepid water

2 eggs

4 cups all-purpose flour

## Directions

- Preheat oven to 375 degrees.
- Mix warm milk, butter, sugar and salt. Let cool to lukewarm.
- Mix yeast with tepid water, letting it dissolve and start to bubble.
- Add yeast and eggs to the milk mixture.
- Add flour 1 cup at a time and mix until dough is formed. You may have to pour mixture on a floured board and add remaining flour by hand until it is stiff enough to handle.
- Knead dough for several minutes, until bubbles form under the surface.
- Place in lightly greased bowl. Cover tightly so air cannot enter and let rise until doubled in size.
- Punch down and let rise again.
- Turn onto a board and let rest a minute, then roll and cut into desired shapes for dinner rolls.
- Place in lightly greased pan, let rise until size is doubled.
- Bake about 15 minutes or until golden brown
- Brush tops with butter.

Note: The secret to making light rolls is to mix properly, not too much flour, knead thoroughly and let rise slowly. Do not rush the process.

# Breakfasts

# PUMPKIN PIE PANCAKES

## Ingredients

- 1/2 cup all-purpose flour
- 1/2 cup whole wheat flour
- 1 tsp baking powder
- 1/2 tsp baking soda
- 2 tsp ground cinnamon
- 1 tsp ground ginger
- 1/2 tsp allspice
- 1/4 cup Splenda®
- 1 large egg
- 2/3 cup canned pumpkin
- 1 Tbsp molasses
- 3/4 cup buttermilk

## Directions

- In a medium bowl, combine flours, baking powder, baking soda, spices and sweetener.
- In a separate bowl, beat egg and add pumpkin, molasses and buttermilk. Mix until thoroughly combined.
- Pour liquid ingredients into dry ingredients and stir until batter forms. Batter will be slightly thick. Letting batter stand for up to 5 minutes results in a lighter pancake.
- Lightly spray skillet or griddle with cooking spray and place over medium heat. Pour 1/4 cup of batter per pancake onto skillet and spread into a 4-inch circle.
- Cook pancake for 3-4 minutes on the first side or until top begins to bubble and bottom is browned.
- Flip pancake and cook for an additional 2-3 minutes.
- Serve with maple syrup or applesauce.

# CREAMED EGGS AND MUSHROOMS

Yield: 4 servings

## Ingredients

1 pkg fresh mushrooms, quartered

4 green onions, sliced

6 hard boiled eggs, sliced

1/2 cup butter or olive oil

1/4 cup flour

2 cups fat free milk

## Directions

- Make a white sauce with butter, flour and milk. Set aside.
- Sauté mushrooms in remaining oil or butter.
- Add sliced green onions and cook 2 more minutes.
- Mix together the white sauce with eggs, and mushroom mixture.
- Season to taste with salt and pepper.

This is very good served over Angel Biscuits (page 28) or toast.

# BROWN PALACE SCONES

*I went to "High Tea" at the famous Brown Palace Hotel in Denver. These scones were served and at that time the recipe was shared. I served my granddaughters these scones with tea at my home and they thoroughly enjoyed the treat.*

## Ingredients

1 cup butter (2 sticks)

1 cup granulated sugar

8 cups all-purpose flour

1 Tbsp baking powder

6 eggs

2 cups buttermilk

## Directions

- Preheat oven to 380 degees.
- Cream together butter and sugar until light and fluffy.
- Add flour and mix on low speed until combined, scraping bowl down occasionally.
- Add buttermilk and eggs at once and mix on low speed for 30 seconds or until combined.
- Turn mixer to highest speed for 15 seconds.
- Chill dough in the refrigerator for at least 1 hour.
- Turn dough out onto floured surface and roll out to approximately 1 1/2 inch thick.
- Cut into circles and place onto baking sheet. (Egg wash and sprinkle with sugar (if desired.)
- Let dough rise for 45 minutes. Bake for 14 -16 minutes or until golden.
- Serve with Devonshire cream (available at most gourmet stores).

Note: This process works best using a Kitchen Aid type mixer with a paddle attachment.

# ANGEL BISCUITS

Yield: 3 dozen

## Ingredients

1 package dry yeast

2 Tbsp warm water

2 cups buttermilk

5 cups flour

1/4 cup sugar

2 tsp baking powder

1 tsp baking soda

1 tsp salt

1 cup shortening

## Directions

- Preheat oven to 400 degrees.
- Combine yeast and warm water; let stand 5 minutes or until bubbly.
- Add buttermilk to yeast mixture and set aside.
- Combine dry ingredients in a large bowl. Cut in shortening until mixture resembles coarse crumbs.
- Add buttermilk mixture, mixing with a fork until dry ingredients are moistened.
- Turn dough out on a floured surface, and knead lightly about 3 or 4 times. Roll dough to 1/2 inch thickness; cut into rounds with a 2 inch cutter.
- Place on lightly greased baking sheet. Bake for 10-12 min.

# KATY'S PANCAKES

Yield: 1 or 2 servings

## Ingredients

  1/2 cup flour
  1/2 cup milk
  2 eggs lightly beaten
  pinch nutmeg
  1/4 cup butter

## Directions

- Preheat oven to 425 degrees
- Mix all ingredients together except butter.
- Melt butter in oven-safe skillet over medium heat
- When skillet is evenly hot, pour in batter.
- Bake for 15 minutes or until brown and puffed up like a soufflé.
- Drizzle with honey or sprinkle with powdered sugar.

---

# FRENCH TOAST CASSEROLE

*This dish needs to be refrigerated at least 8 hours to attain the correct texture. Do not refrigerate for longer than 24 hours, or the bread will disintegrate. Assemble the topping just before baking.*

## Ingredients

  1 -16 oz French bread, sliced 1/2 inch or Texas toast
  1 Tbsp unsalted butter, softened
  8 large eggs
  2 cups whole milk
  2 cups half and half
  1 Tbsp sugar
  2 tsp vanilla

1/2 tsp ground cinnamon

1/2 tsp ground nutmeg

## Topping

12 Tbsp unsalted butter, softened

3 Tbsp corn syrup

1 1/3 cups light brown sugar, packed

1 1/2 cups pecans or walnuts, coarsely chopped

## Directions

- Arrange the bread in a single layer on two baking sheets. Bake until dry and light golden brown, about 25 minutes on racks in middle of the oven. Transfer to a wire rack and cool completely.
- Grease bottom and sides of a 9x13" baking dish with butter. Layer the dried bread tightly in the prepared dish. (you should have two layers)
- Whisk eggs, milk, half and half, sugar, vanilla, cinnamon and nutmeg together in a large bowl and pour evenly over bread, pressing lightly to submerge.
- Cover tightly with plastic wrap and refrigerate for at least 8 hours.
- Mix butter, corn syrup, and brown sugar together until smooth and fully incorporated.
- Stir in pecans.
- Remove casserole from refrigerator and discard plastic wrap. Spoon the topping over the casserole. Spread into an even layer using rubber spatula.
- When ready to bake, adjust an oven rack to the middle position and preheat oven to 350 degrees.
- Place baking dish on cookie sheet and bake until puffed and golden, about 60 minutes. Cool for 10 minutes before serving.

Option: During the holidays when eggnog is available, I substitute 2 cups egg beaters for eggs, a quart of prepared eggnog for the milk and half and half. Omit sugar. Follow remaining directions as printed. Makes a great holiday brunch or breakfast dish.

# GRIDDLECAKES

*Recipe from Semret Clark*

## Ingredients

1 1/4 cups flour

1 Tbsp vegetable oil

1 1/2 tsp baking powder

1 egg, well beaten

3/4 tsp salt

1 Tbsp sugar

1 cup milk

## Directions

- Sift flour, salt and sugar together. Combine egg and milk. Add milk and egg to flour along with oil.
- Mix until flour is dampened. Batter will be lumpy.
- Bake on a greased griddle until browned on both sides.
- Serve with bacon and maple syrup.

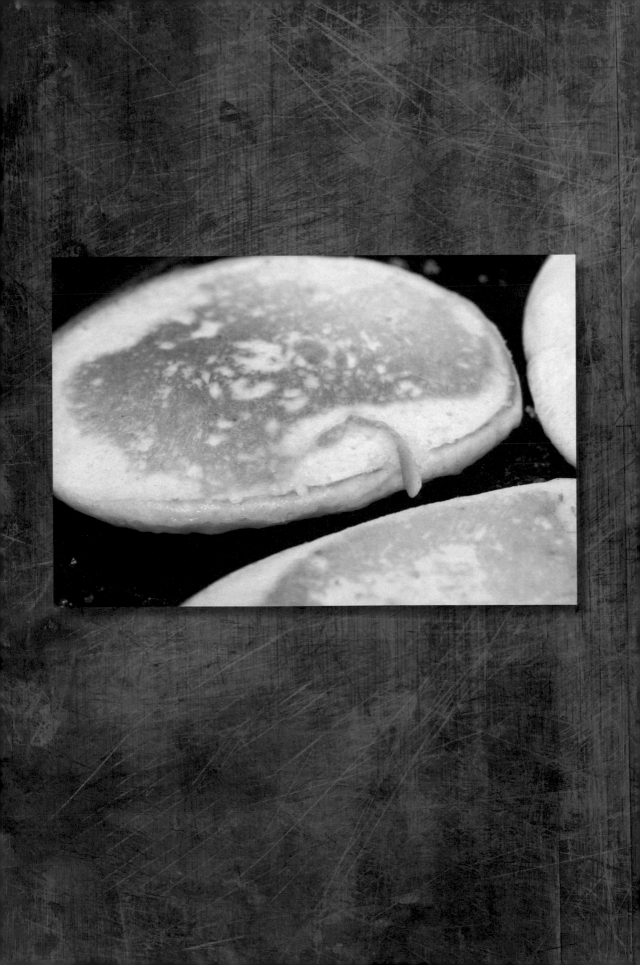

# Salads

# STRAWBERRY SPINACH SALAD

Yield: 8 servings

## Ingredients

Dressing

> poppy seed dressing (can substitute a low carbohydrate poppy seed dressing)
>
> 1/3 cup sugar or Splenda®
>
> 1/4 cup cider vinegar
>
> 3 Tbsp vegetable oil
>
> 1 Tbsp poppy seeds
>
> 1/4 tsp paprika
>
> 1/4 tsp Worcestershire sauce

Salad

- 1 pint strawberries cut in quarters
- 1 pound fresh spinach, trimmed, torn (may use part assorted greens)

## Directions

Dressing

- Combine sugar, vinegar and oil into a saucepan. Cook mixture over medium low heat until the sugar dissolves.
- Remove from the heat and let mixture cool slightly.
- Stir into saucepan the poppy seeds, paprika and Worcestershire sauce.

Salad

- In a large bowl, mix together greens and strawberries.
- Pour dressing over greens and strawberries and toss gently.
- Serve immediately.

Optional: Add grilled chicken to make this a main dish salad.

# GRAPE BROCCOLI SALAD

Yield: 3 (1 cup) servings

## Ingredients

1 cup fresh broccoli florets

3/4 cup seedless red grapes, halved

1/3 cup chopped celery

1/3 cup chopped green onions

1/3 cup sliced water chestnuts

1/4 cup raisins

1/2 cup fat-free plain yogurt

2 Tbsp reduced fat mayonnaise

1 tsp honey

## Directions

- In a large bowl, combine the broccoli, grapes, celery, onions, water chestnuts and raisins.
- In a small bowl, combine yogurt, mayonnaise and honey.
- Pour mixture from small bowl over broccoli mixture and mix well.
- Cover and refrigerate for at least 1 hour or until chilled.

## Nutrition

Calories: 129 kcal;  Fat: 4g; Saturated Fat: 1g; Cholesterol: 4mg; Sodium: 127mg;  Carbohydrate: 24g;  Fiber : 3g, Protein: 3g
Diabetic Exchange: 1 fruit, 1/2 starch, 1/2 fat

# PECAN CRANBERRY SALAD

*Low-calorie gelatin thickens, but doesn't set this tangy relish.*

Yield: 10 (1/3 cup) servings

## Ingredients

    1 (12 oz) package fresh cranberries
    1 cup water
    1/2 cup sugar
    1 (4 serving size) package sugar-free cranberry or raspberry
    flavored gelatin
    1 (15 1/4 oz) can crushed pineapple in juice
    1/3 cup pecans, coarsely chopped and toasted

## Directions

- In a large saucepan combine cranberries and water.
- Bring mixture to a boil over medium high heat.
- Reduce heat and bring to a simmer, uncovered; cook for 3 minutes or until berries pop.
- Remove saucepan from heat.
- In a medium bowl add sugar and gelatin; stir until mixture is dissolved.
- Add pineapple (with juice).
- Combine all ingredients into a serving bowl.
- Cover and refrigerate approximately 6 hours or until mixture has thickened.
- Sprinkle with pecans before serving.

## Nutrition

    Calories: 160kcal; Fat: 3g; Saturated Fat: 0g; Cholesterol: 0mg;
    Sodium: 27mg; Carbohydrates: 20g; Fiber: 2g; Protein: 1g
    Diabetic Exchanges: 1/2 fruit, 1 other carbohydrate 1/2 fat,
    1 carbohydrate

# CANTALOUPE and WATERMELON SALAD

*Looks beautiful served in a large glass bowl or serving dish.*

## Ingredients:

1/2 medium-sized watermelon

1 whole large cantaloupe

1/2 cup fresh basil, chopped

feta cheese (optional)

fresh mint sprigs

## Directions

- Remove watermelon from rind and cut into cubes.
- Remove seeds and outer peel from cantaloupe and cut into cubes.
- Mix together with fresh basil.
- Sprinkle with feta cheese, if desired.
- Garnish with fresh mint sprigs.

## Notes

# Soups

*Soups, stews and chili dishes allow creativity with simplicity and are packed with nutrients. They can be used as main dishes which are generally filling and less expensive than meat meals. I find that soups are easy and quick to create with whatever vegetables might be on hand. It's a good idea to stock canned 'no salt added' beans, such as black, pinto, red, kidney, navy, cannellini, and garbanzo. Any of these can be added to soup to give body, fiber, and protein. RO\*TEL tomatoes are a great addition because they provide a pleasant, spicy kick. Frozen mixed vegetables can be used to save time and fresh or frozen spinach or kale adds color and variety to soups.*

# SAM'S GREEN CHILI

## Ingredients

1 pound lean pork, cubed

1/4 cup vegetable oil

1/2 cup flour

1 medium onion, chopped

2 cloves garlic or 1/2 tsp garlic powder

3 cups fresh green chilies roasted *or* 1 can (28 oz) Hatch's chilies, diced

1/2 tsp oregano

1/2 tsp cilantro

1/2 tsp cumin

1 can (15 oz) peeled tomatoes

1 can (8 oz) tomatillos

## Directions

- Dredge pork cubes in flour.
- Over medium heat, pour oil into skillet and add pork cubes.
- Allow to brown and remove from skillet, (scraping any excess flour and meat pieces) and place into a large pot.
- Add onion and garlic to skillet over medium heat; add chilies and remaining spices. Sauté for approximately 5 minutes.
- Remove vegetables and spices from heat and add to pork.
- Add tomatoes (smash by hand as you put in the pot) and 2 cups of water, or enough to cover the meat mixture.
- Bring to boil, reduce heat to low and cook for approximately 3 hours. Stir occasionally to prevent sticking.
- Season to taste with salt and pepper.
- Serve chili over rice, burritos, or as a soup.

Note: When selecting peppers, you can choose your desired degree of heat (mild, medium or hot).

# SAVORY KALE, CANNELLINI BEAN, and POTATO SOUP

## Ingredients

2 Tbsp extra-virgin olive oil

1 onion, diced

3/4 cup carrots, diced

4 cloves garlic, minced

3 cups low-sodium chicken broth

2 cups water

3 potatoes, halved and sliced

1/2 tsp fresh rosemary, chopped

1/2 tsp fresh sage, chopped

1/2 tsp fresh thyme, chopped

1 (16 oz) can cannellini beans, rinsed and drained

2 cups kale leaves, finely chopped

1 small red chili pepper, seeded and finely chopped

ground black pepper to taste

## Directions

- Heat the olive oil in a large Dutch oven over medium heat.
- Cook and stir onion until softened and translucent, about 5 minutes.
- Stir in carrots and garlic; cook for 5 more minutes.
- Pour in chicken broth and water; stir in potatoes, rosemary, sage, and thyme.
- Bring to a boil over high heat. Reduce heat to medium-low, cover and simmer until potatoes are tender, about 20 minutes.
- Add cannellini beans, kale, chili pepper, and black pepper.
- Cover and simmer for 30 minutes; serve.

## Nutrition

Calories: 262kcal; Fat: 5.4g; Carbohydrate: 38.8g; Protein: 8.2g; Cholesterol: 2mg; Sodium: 245mg

# POTATO CORN CHOWDER

Yield: 6 servings

## Ingredients

1 medium onion, chopped

2 stalks celery, chopped

2 Tbsp butter

1 1/2 pounds Yukon gold potatoes (about 5 medium) peeled and cubed

1 can (15 oz) cream style corn

1 can (15 oz) whole kernel corn

1 (12 oz) can fat free evaporated milk

salt and pepper to taste

## Directions

- In a medium pan, sauté onions and celery in butter until tender.
- Fill a large saucepan with water; add potatoes, and bring to a boil over medium high heat.
- Cook potatoes for about 10-15 minutes until fork tender, remove from the heat, drain, reserving 1 cup of potato water.
- Add corn, milk, salt and pepper and reserved potato water and onion mixture.
- If soup is too thick add the fat free milk to desired consistency.

Option: 1/2 pound bacon strips, chopped and cooked crisp can be added, if desired.

## Nutrition

Calories: 271kcal; Fat: 11mg; Cholesterol: 3mg; Sodium: 555mg; Fiber: 2g; Protein: 10g. *

* Without bacon, the fat and sodium grams will be less.

# BEAN SOUP WITH KALE

Yield: 8-10 (1 1/2 cup) servings

## Ingredients

1 Tbsp olive oil or canola oil

8 large garlic cloves, crushed or minced

1 medium yellow onion, chopped

4 cups raw kale, chopped

4 cups low-fat, low-sodium chicken or vegetable broth

2 (15 oz) cans white beans, such as cannellini or navy, undrained

1 (10 oz) can RO*TEL tomatoes

2 tsp dried Italian herb seasoning

salt and pepper

1 cup parsley, chopped

## Directions

- In a large pot, heat olive oil over medium heat.
- Add the garlic and onion; sauté until soft.
- Add the kale and sauté, stirring until wilted.
- Add 3 cups of broth, 2 cups of beans, the tomatoes, herbs, and salt and pepper (season to taste).
- Bring to a simmer for 5 minutes.
- In a blender or food processor, add the remaining beans and broth and blend until smooth.
- Stir into the soup to thicken.
- Bring to a simmer for 15 minutes.
- Ladle soup into bowls; sprinkle with chopped parsley.

## Nutrition

Calories: 182 kcal; Fat: 2.5g; Carbohydrate : 31g; Protein 11g; Cholesterol: 0mg Sodium: 220mg

# THREE BEAN MINESTRONE SOUP

Yield: 8-10 (1 1/2 cup) servings

## Ingredients

4 Tbsp olive oil

1 large onion, peeled and diced

2 medium carrots, peeled and diced

2 stalks celery, diced

1 (15 oz) can cannellini beans, drained and rinsed, no salt added

1 (15 oz) can pinto beans, drained and rinsed, no salt added

1 (15 oz) can kidney beans, drained and rinsed, no salt added

8 cups water

2 medium white potatoes, diced

2 yellow summer squash, diced

1 (1 lb) package frozen soup mix vegetables with cut okra

1 (27 oz) can diced canned tomatoes *or* 1 (15 oz) can diced tomatoes and 1 (10 oz) can RO*TEL tomatoes

1 tsp each: oregano, rosemary or other herbs of choice

4 cups baby spinach or kale cut into small pieces

1 cup dry pasta of your choice

## Directions

- In a large stock pot over low heat, combine the olive oil and onions and sauté until soft.
- Add carrots and cook for 3 minutes.
- Add celery, beans, water, frozen vegetables and potatoes and cook for about 20 minutes.
- Add tomatoes (with juice) and squash.
- Add herbs, cover and simmer for about 30 minutes.
- Add spinach and pasta into pot and cook for an additional 5 -7 minutes.
- Season soup to taste with salt and pepper.

## Nutrition

Calories: 317kcal; Total fat: 16g; Cholesterol: 4mg; Sodium: 480mg; Carbohydrate: 35g; Fiber: 10g; Protein: 12g; Potassium: 737mg.

# BUTTERNUT SQUASH SOUP

Yield: 4 servings as a main dish; 8 servings as a side dish

## Ingredients

1 Tbsp butter

1 large onion, chopped

1 medium-size butternut squash, peeled and diced (2 1/2 pounds)

1 large cooking apple, diced (peel on)

3 Tbsp all-purpose flour

1 1/2 tsp curry powder

1/8 tsp ground nutmeg

2 (14-ounce) cans reduced-sodium chicken broth

1 cup nonfat milk

1 Tbsp orange zest

1/4 cup orange juice

1/4 tsp white pepper

1/4 cup freshly chopped parsley (optional)

## Directions

- In a 3 or 4 quart large saucepan, melt butter over medium heat.
- Sauté onion until tender, approximately 5 minutes.
- Add squash and apple to saucepan and sauté for an additional 5 minutes.
- Stir in flour, curry powder and nutmeg and cook for 5 more minutes.

continued >>

- Stir in broth, milk, orange zest, orange juice and white pepper.
- Cover and simmer for 20 minutes or until squash is tender.
- Puree soup in a blender or a food processor (a blender works best) in small batches (about 1 1/2 cups at a time) until smooth.
- Garnish soup with parsley and orange zest, if desired.

## Nutrition

**Serving size 8:** Calories: 130kcal; Fat: 2.5g; Saturated Fat: 1.5g; Cholesterol: 5mg; Sodium: 80mg; Carbohydrate: 25g; Dietary Fiber: 5g; Protein: 4g

**Serving size 4:** Calories: 270 kcal; Fat: 5g; Saturated Fat: 2.5g; Cholesterol: 15mg; Sodium: 160mg; Carbohydrate: 51g; Dietary Fiber: 11g; Protein: 9g

# Notes

# Main Dishes

My first place of employment in Denver, Colorado was a Jewish
hospital for asthmatic children. Coming from Oklahoma, I had no
previous exposure to the Jewish dietary laws; it was a whole new world
of menu planning. That was the beginning of my journey learning about
different cultures and food habits; how to prepare the dishes. I also appre-
ciated the many different options to share with my family. Cheese blintzes,
potato pancakes or latkes, and matzo ball soup are a few of my favorites
and I continue to serve them to my family.

# SPAGHETTI CHEESE CASSEROLE

*This is Charmetra Robert's favorite—it's quick and easy!*

## Ingredients

1/4 lb spaghetti

3 Tbsp butter or margarine

2 Tbsp onion

3 Tbsp flour

1 (16 oz) can diced tomatoes

1 tsp salt

1/4 tsp pepper

1/4 tsp sugar

1/4 cup grated cheese

4 wieners cut into 1 inch pieces

## Directions

- Preheat oven to 350 degrees.
- Cook spaghetti according to package directions.
- Melt butter or margarine and lightly brown the onions.
- Stir in flour; add tomatoes, salt, pepper, sugar and cheese.
- Remove from heat; stir in cooked spaghetti and wieners.
- Sprinkle more grated cheese on top and bake 30 minutes.

# TEXAS RED

*Recipe from Yolanda Anderson*

## Ingredients

2 Tbsp vegetable oil

2 pounds stewing beef, cubed

1 cup chopped onions

1 green bell pepper, seeded and chopped

1 clove garlic, minced

1 (12 oz) can tomato paste

2 jalapeno peppers, seeded and diced

1 1/2 Tbsp chili powder

1/2 tsp crushed red pepper

1/2 tsp salt

1/2 tsp oregano

1/2 tsp cumin

1 (15 1/2 oz) can pinto beans, drained

## Directions

- Using a large heavy pan, heat oil and brown beef.
- Add onions, bell peppers, garlic and sauté with beef for about 5 minutes.
- Add all remaining ingredients except beans cover and simmer 1 1/2 hours.
- Add beans and simmer for 30 minutes longer.

---

# SLOW COOKER MEXICAN CASSEROLE

*Recipe from Belinda Garner Sparks*

## Ingredients

5 (3 oz) chicken breast, thawed

1 (10 oz) can chopped green chilies

2 (10 oz) cans chopped tomatoes

1 package taco seasoning

## Directions

- Put all the ingredients into slow cooker; cook on low for 8 hours or high for 3-4 hours.
- Serve on tortillas with cheese and sour cream.

# CABBAGE AND NOODLES

## Ingredients

1 medium cabbage, shredded

1 large sweet onion, sliced thin

1/4 cup butter or olive oil

1 (15 oz) can diced tomatoes in juice

1 (16 oz.) package wide egg noodles

1 qt. chicken stock or vegetable broth

## Directions

- Cook pasta in chicken stock.
- Heat butter or oil in skillet over medium heat.
- Sauté cabbage and onions until tender and add tomatoes.
- Drain pasta and save broth.
- Add cabbage and onion mixture to noodles.
- Season with salt and pepper to taste. If needed, add some of the reserve broth.

# SLOW COOKER PASTA FAGIOLA

## Ingredients

1 lb lean ground beef, browned and drained.

1/2 large red onion, chopped

1 cup carrots, chopped

2 celery stalks, sliced

1 (15 oz) can kidney beans drained and rinsed

1 (15 oz) can white beans drained and rinsed

2 (14 oz) cans diced tomatoes with juice

1 (16 oz) jar pasta sauce

4 cups beef broth

2 tsp oregano

1 Tbsp tabasco sauce

1/2 cup dry pasta, to add at end of cooking time.

## Directions

- Use a large slow cooker or cut recipe in half.
- Place onions, carrots and celery in slow cooker.
- Drain and rinse beans and add to slow cooker.
- Add tomatoes and pasta sauce.
- Add beef broth, oregano and tabasco sauce.
- Stir in meat.
- Cover and cook on low for 8 hours or on high for 4 hours.
- Stir in dry pasta, cover and cook another hour or until pasta is done.
- Add salt and pepper to taste.

# ENCHILIDAS

## Ingredients

1 lb ground beef

1 (15 oz) can refried beans

1 (15 oz) can enchilada sauce

8 oz sour cream

8 oz shredded Monterey Jack cheese

10 - 12 tortillas

## Directions:

- Preheat oven to 350 degrees.
- Brown ground beef, drain.
- Mix in refried beans and 1/2 can of enchilada sauce and simmer.
- Roll into tortillas and place in baking dish.
- Top with sour cream, Monterey Jack cheese and remaining enchilada sauce.
- Bake for 20 minutes.

# OVEN or GRILLED BBQ RIBS

*Shared by Yaa Shanti*

## Ingredients

2 racks baby back ribs

1 bottle (2 liter) Dr. Pepper

Kosher salt and black pepper to taste

1 Tbsp chili powder

1 cup water

1/2 Tbsp olive oil

1/2 onion, minced

1 clove garlic, minced

1/2 cup catsup

2 Tbsp Worcestershire sauce

2 Tbsp apple cider vinegar

1/4 tsp cayenne pepper

## Directions

- Place ribs in roasting pan; pour enough soda to cover, saving 1/2 cup for BBQ sauce.
- Sprinkle 2 Tbsp salt over ribs and let set for 2 hours or overnight in refrigerator.
- Remove ribs from liquid, discard liquid, pat dry and sprinkle with chili powder.
- Add water, cover tightly and bake for 2 hours at 350 degrees.
- While ribs are in oven, make barbeque sauce with remaining ingredients. Simmer for 15-20 minutes until it thickens.
- Remove ribs from pan and place on grill over charcoal for 10-15 minutes on each side until smoky and baste with BBQ sauce.

### GRILL OPTION:

- Follow directions above through step 2.
- Precook ribs for approximately 15 minutes.
- Place over hot charcoal on grill to complete cooking.
- Baste with Myle's BBQ sauce (page 142).

# OVEN FRIED CHICKEN

*Diabetic Friendly*

## Ingredients

Boneless thighs or split breasts approximately 3 ounces each

|  | 6 pieces | 25 pieces |
| --- | --- | --- |
| non-fat milk | 1 cup | 1 quart |
| thyme | 1 tsp | 4 tsp |
| garlic powder | 1 tsp | 4 tsp |
| onion powder | 1 tsp | 4 tsp |
| paprika | 1 tsp | 4 tsp |
| black pepper | 1 tsp | 4 tsp |
| red pepper | 1/4 tsp | 2 tsp |
| salt | 1/2 tsp | 1 Tbsp |
| whole wheat flour | 1 cup | 1 quart |
| parsley | 1 tsp | 1/4 cup |
| olive oil | 1 Tbsp | 1/4 cup |

## Directions

- Preheat oven to 400 degrees.
- Place chicken pieces in milk.
- In a large bowl, combine all remaining ingredients.
- Dip each chicken piece in flour mixture making sure each piece is well coated. Discard remaining flour.
- Place chicken in shallow baking pan that has been sprayed with non-stick spray.
- Brush chicken pieces lightly with olive oil. Bake for 45 minutes or until chicken juices run clear.

# ARA'S BAKED BALSAMIC CHICKEN

*Diabetic Friendly! A really great dish; the rosemary makes it exceptional.*

## Ingredients

4 chicken breast (boneless, skinless)

1/4 cup balsamic vinegar

2 Tbsp olive oil

spices: salt, pepper, rosemary, onion powder, garlic powder

## Directions

- Preheat oven to 350 degrees.
- In a large bowl combine balsamic vinegar, pinch of salt, pepper, onion, garlic and rosemary; mix well.
- Add chicken breast and mix, so that chicken is fully covered with the mixture. Let marinade for about 20-30 minutes.
- Place chicken in a casserole or an oven safe dish, adding leftover marinade.
- Bake uncovered for 20 minutes or until chicken juices run clear.

Note: Remember to wash hands each time after handling chicken.

# TURKEY LETTUCE WRAPS

*Diabetic Friendly*

## Ingredients

1 tsp sesame oil

1 pound extra-lean ground turkey

1/2 cup green onions, sliced

2 Tbsp fresh ginger, minced

1 can (8 ounce) water chestnuts, chopped

1 tsp light soy sauce

1/4 cup fresh cilantro, chopped

12 large lettuce leaves, Bibb or butter

## Directions

- Heat oil in large skillet over medium-high heat.
- Add turkey, onion and ginger. Cook 7 minutes, breaking meat up with back of spoon.
- Add water chestnuts and soy sauce.
- Cook until meat is browned and no longer pink.
- Remove from heat; stir in cilantro.
- Spoon 1/4 cup mixture into a lettuce leaf. Add optional toppings; roll up.

*Optional toppings:* chopped mint leaves; chopped dry roasted peanuts.
*Serving suggestion:* Serve with mixed fresh fruit salad.

## Nutrition

Calories: 102 kcal; Total Fat: 2g; Saturated Fat: 1g;
Carbohydrate: 6g; Fiber: 1g; Protein: 18g; Sodium: 87mg

# FISH TACOS

*This recipe is from* Simply Colorado Too.

## Ingredients

Tacos

> 1 lb grilled white fish
>
> 2 cups cabbage, shredded
>
> 1 avocado, cut into 8 slices
>
> 8 (6-inch) flour tortillas
>
> juice of 1 lime

Cilantro Sauce

> 1/2 cup reduced-fat ranch salad dressing
>
> 1/2 cup plain fat free yogurt
>
> 1/2 cup trimmed fresh cilantro leaves
>
> 2 Tbsp canned chopped green chilies

## Directions

Tacos

- For tacos, cut fish into eight 2 ounce portions.
- Layer 1/4 cup cabbage, 2 ounce fish and 1 slice of avocado in each tortilla; fold over to enclose the filling.
- Top each taco with some of the sauce and drizzle with lime juice.

Cilantro Sauce

- Combine salad dressing, yogurt, cilantro and chilies in a blender or food processor and process until smooth.

Note: Coleslaw mix may be used for shredded cabbage. Fresh jalapeno peppers may be used in sauce for an extra kick.

# PIGS' FEET

*Although not considered a healthy choice, it is one of those foods that can be eaten on special occasions. This is a great way to prepare them.*
*Recipe from D Taylor*

## Ingredients

3 or 4 whole pigs' feet

1 cup vinegar

1 (10 oz) can RO*TEL tomatoes

1 (12 oz) can tomato sauce

1-2 bell peppers, chopped

1-2 onions sliced

3-4 garlic cloves

salt and pepper to taste

## Directions

- Preheat oven to 300 degrees.
- Wash pigs' feet and place in roasting pan. Cover with all ingredients.
- Bake overnight or until tender.

# MOUTH-WATERING OVEN FRIED FISH

*Diabetic Friendly*

## Ingredients

2 lbs. fish fillets (any type)

1 Tbsp lemon juice, fresh

1/4 cup skim milk or 1 percent buttermilk

2 drops hot pepper sauce

1 tsp garlic, minced

1/4 tsp salt

1/4 tsp onion powder

1/2 cup cornflake crumbs or bread crumbs

1 lemon, cut in wedges

## Directions

- Preheat oven to 475 degrees.
- Brush fillets with lemon juice.
- Dip fillets in milk and hot pepper combination and let soak briefly.
- Combine salt and onion powder with cornflake crumbs and place on a plate.
- Coat fillets with the cornflake mixture on both sides. Let stand briefly until coating sticks to each side of fish.
- Arrange on lightly oiled shallow baking dish.
- Bake 20 minutes on middle rack without turning. Fish should flake easily with a fork when done.
- Serve with fresh lemon.

## Nutrition

Calories: 183; Fat: 2g; Saturated Fat: less than 1g;
Cholesterol: 80 mg; Sodium: 325mg

# BACON GRILLED FISH

*My son, George, enjoys fishing. This is his recipe for smoked fish with bacon.*

## Ingredients:

fish fillets, your choice of a firm white fish such as bass, perch, etc.

bacon, thin sliced (one slice per fish fillet)

garlic powder, to taste

pepper, to taste

kosher salt, to taste

olive oil or butter

white wine (*optional*)

## Directions:

- Soak your favorite wood chips in water.
- Build a fire with charcoal and allow to burn down.
- Prepare fish fillets: lightly season with garlic powder, pepper and kosher salt.
- Carefully stretch a slice of bacon diagonally around each fish filet and fasten with toothpick.
- Once the coals are gray, add wood chips.
- When fire is low and smoky, do not place fish directly over coals but place on grill and away from fire.
- Allow to smoke for approximately 1 hour.
- The bacon keeps fish from sticking but if necessary, move fish back to hotter area of grill for bacon to get crisp.
- Baste with olive oil or butter mixed with white wine (*optional*).
- Rotate fish from less heat to more heat until desired degree of doneness and smoke flavor.

# ALMOND CHICKEN STIR-FRY

*Diabetic Friendly*

## Ingredients

1 lb boneless skinless chicken breast, cut into thin strips

3/4 cup almonds, sliced

1 Tbsp canola oil

1 (16 oz) frozen broccoli stir-fry vegetables

1 Tbsp cornstarch

1 Tbsp brown sugar

1/2 tsp ground ginger

1/3 cup pineapple juice, unsweetened

1/3 cup reduced-sodium soy sauce

brown rice, cooked and served hot, optional

## Directions

- In a large nonstick skillet or wok, stir-fry chicken and almonds in hot oil for 2 minutes.
- Add vegetables and reduce heat to low; cover and cook for 4 minutes or until vegetables are tender and chicken is no longer pink.
- In small bowl, combine cornstarch, brown sugar and ginger.
- Stir in pineapple juice and soy sauce until smooth.
- Stir into chicken mixture and bring to boil; cook and stir for 2 minutes or until thickened.
- Serve with rice if desired.

## Nutrition

One serving (1 cup stir fry mixture calculated with rice)
Calories: 278 kcal; Fat: 11g; Saturated Fat: 1g; Cholesterol: 54mg;
Sodium: 708mg; Carbohydrate: 17g; Fiber: 3g; Protein: 25g

# TURKEY MEATLOAF or MEAT BALLS

*Diabetic Friendly*

## Ingredients

- 1 lb ground turkey
- 1 medium onion, chopped
- 1 medium bell pepper, chopped
- 1/2 cup quick-cooking oatmeal
- 1 tsp Italian seasoning
- 2 cloves garlic, minced
- 1 tsp Mrs. Dash® seasoning
- 1 tsp Creole seasoning
- 1 egg or equivalent egg substitute
- 1/4 cup skim milk

## Directions

- Preheat oven to 375 degrees; prepare baking sheet by spraying with non-stick cooking spray.
- Mix all ingredients in a large bowl.
- Shape into meat balls using a size 40 scoop or tablespoon and place on baking sheet.
- Bake 20-40 minutes or until done.

## Nutrition

Calories: 160 kcal; Fat: 7g; Saturated Fat: 2g; Trans Fat: 0g; Cholesterol: 60mg; Sodium: 105mg; Total Carbohydrate: 8g; Dietary fiber: 2g; Sugars: 3g; Protein: 16g

# SESAME VEGETABLE STIR-FRY

*The sesame oil and soy sauce enhances the flavor.*
*Diabetic Friendly*

## Ingredients

1 lb broccoli

1/4 lb fresh snow peas, strings removed

1 red onion, sliced

3 Tbsp sesame oil

1 red bell pepper, cut into 1/4-inch strips

2 tsp minced garlic

1/4 cup reduced sodium soy sauce

1/2 Tbsp sesame seeds

## Directions

- Trim broccoli leaving 1 inch of stem. Cut the remaining stems into small slices.
- Place broccoli and snow peas in a saucepan of boiling water and cook for 1 minute. Drain and rinse immediately with cold water. Drain again and set aside.
- Heat a large wok or large skillet over high heat.
- Add sesame oil, blanched broccoli, red onion, red bell pepper and garlic. Stir-fry for 1 minute. Add the blanched snow peas and soy sauce; stir-fry 1 minute longer. Remove from heat and stir in sesame seeds.

## Nutrition

Calories: 191 kcal; Fat: 11.4g; Carbs: 16.9g Protein: 7g; Sodium: 1258mg.

Optional: can be served over brown rice or quinoa, which will increase the carbs and protein nutritional values. See product packaging for cooking directions and nutritional information per serving.

# BAKED PORK CHOPS

*Diabetic Friendly*

## Ingredients

6 lean center-cut pork chops, 1/2-inch thick

1 medium onion, thinly sliced

1/2 cup green pepper, sliced

1/2 cup red pepper, sliced

1/8 tsp black pepper

1/4 tsp salt.

## Directions

- Preheat oven to 375 degrees.
- Trim fat from pork chops. Place chops in a 13 by 9-inch baking pan.
- Spread onion and peppers on top of chops. Sprinkle with pepper and salt. Refrigerate for 1 hour.
- Cover pan and bake 30 minutes. Uncover, turn chops and continue baking for an additional 15 minutes or until no pink remains.  Garnish with fresh parsley.

## Nutrition

Calories: 170 kcal; Fat: 8g; Saturated Fat: 3g; Cholesterol: 61mg; Sodium: 135mg

# SAUCY TURKEY MEATBALLS

## Ingredients

1 1/2 pounds lean ground turkey

1 cup oatmeal

3/4 cup fat free milk

1 medium onion, chopped

2 cloves garlic minced

1 tsp salt

1 tsp chili powder

1/2 tsp pepper

## Sauce

1 cup catsup

1 cup Splenda®

1/4 cup chopped onion

2 Tbsp liquid smoke

1 tsp garlic, minced

## Directions

- Preheat oven to 350 degrees.
- Mix turkey with ingredients for meat balls. Shape into balls and place on baking sheet coated with nonstick cooking spray. Bake 10-15 minutes.
- Mix sauce ingredients well and pour over meat balls. Bake 30-35 minutes until meat is no longer pink. Serving size: 3 meatballs.

Brining:

Brining is a great way to add moisture to turkey, roasting chicken, and/or other meats. I use 1/2 cup kosher salt, 1/2 cup sugar dissolved in 1 quart of water. Place bird in large pot or a brining bag and cover with the salt solution. Place in refrigerator for at least 8 hours or overnight (no more than overnight). Remove from salt solution, rinse and allow to air dry to assure crisp skin. Cooking bags or roasting pan can be used to cook the bird. Follow package directions or your favorite roasting recipe but do not add salt.

# LEMON GINGER SPRING VEGETABLE STIR-FRY

*Diabetic Friendly*

## Ingredients

3 Tbsp sesame oil

3 Tbsp low sodium soy sauce

2 Tbsp fresh ginger, grated

2 Tbsp lemon peel, grated

1 Tbsp hoisin sauce

16 asparagus spears, diagonally cut in 2 inch lengths (may substitute 1 cup edamame beans if asparagus is not in season)

2 carrots, peeled and sliced diagonally

1 broccoli crown, cut into small florets

2 cups fresh pineapple, chopped

1 red chili pepper, thinly sliced

2 Tbsp water

3 cups fresh baby spinach

1 cup fresh strawberries, quartered

3 cups cooked hot quinoa

## Directions

- Combine in sauté pan sesame oil, soy sauce, ginger, lemon peel and hoisin sauce; heat over medium high heat.
- Add asparagus, carrots, broccoli, pineapple, chili pepper and water. Cover and cook for 2 minutes. Remove cover and continue cooking to desired softness.
- Remove pan from heat and stir in baby spinach and strawberries. Serve over cooked quinoa
- Follow directions on quinoa package for serving size and nutritional content.

Note: Pasta and rice main dishes instead of meat can be a welcome addition and liven up meal plans. They also provide opportunity to try unfamiliar vegetables that might become a mainstay.

## Nutrition

Serving size: 1 1/4 cups; Calories: 210kcal (80kcal from fat);
Total fat: 9g; Saturated fat: 1g; Trans-fat: 0g; Cholesterol: 0g;
Sodium: 390 mg; Potassium: 640 mg; Dietary Fiber: 6g;
Sugars: 10g; Protein: 7g

---

# SOUTHWEST VEGETABLE CHILI

*Diabetic Friendly*

*This recipe was given to me by Sharon Larson. It keeps well, can be frozen and makes a great meatless meal without the turkey or beef.*

Yield: 20 (1 cup) servings

## Ingredients

1 pkg frozen southwest-style mixed vegetables

2 (15 oz) cans kidney beans (no salt added)

2 (15 oz) cans pinto beans (no salt added)

2 (15 oz) cans black beans (no salt added)

2 (10 oz) cans RO*TEL diced tomatoes with cilantro and lime

1 (15 oz) can tomato sauce

1 pkg low sodium taco seasoning mix

1 lb (optional) lean ground beef or turkey

## Directions

- Cook frozen vegetables, add canned vegetables.
- Brown meat and add taco seasoning.
- Mix with vegetables and simmer to blend flavors.
- Serve with grated cheese on the side.

## Nutrition

Calories: 180 kcal; Fat: 4.5 g; Cholesterol: 20 mg; Sodium: 360 mg;
Dietary Fiber: 9g; Carbohydrates: 24g; Protein: 15g

# CHICKEN POT PIE WITH BISCUITS

*This is a great use for leftover rotisserie chicken.*

Yield: 8 servings

## Ingredients

1 Tbsp butter or margarine

1 cup chopped onions (2 medium)

1/4 cup all-purpose flour

1 tsp dried tarragon leaves

1/4 tsp pepper

2 cups chicken broth (from 32 oz carton)

1 cup milk

2 large potatoes, peeled, cubed (about 3 cups)

1 (12 oz) bag frozen peas and carrots

1 (16 oz) can refrigerated buttermilk or original biscuits

2 1/2 cups cubed cooked chicken

## Directions

- Preheat oven to 350 degrees.
- In 4-quart saucepan, melt butter over medium-high heat. Add onions and cook 2 to 3 minutes, stirring frequently, until tender.
- Add cubed potatoes and broth and continue cooking about 5 minutes.
- Stir in peas and carrots. Heat to boiling, stirring occasionally.
- Mix flour with a small amount of milk, stirring with a fork to prevent lumping.
- Add all milk, tarragon and pepper, stir until well blended.
- Cook 8 to 10 minutes, stirring frequently, until vegetables are crisp-tender.
- Meanwhile separate dough into 8 biscuits.
- Stir chicken into vegetable mixture and return to boiling. Remove from heat, spoon into casserole dish.
- Place biscuits around edge of dish, overlapping slightly but leaving hole in center for steam to escape.

continued >>

- Bake 20-25 minutes or until vegetables are tender and biscuits are golden brown. Let stand 5 minutes before serving.

## Nutrition

Calories: 310kcals (Calories from Fat110); Total Fat 12g (Saturated Fat: 4 1/2g; Trans Fat: 1 1/2g); Cholesterol: 70mg; Sodium: 700mg; Carbohydrate: 31g; Dietary Fiber: 3g; Sugars: 6g; Protein: 19g

---

# MEXICAN STYLE STUFFED PEPPERS

## Ingredients

4 large green bell peppers (tops, seeds, and membranes removed)

1 Tbsp olive oil

1/2 cup chopped onion

2 cups cooked rice (preferably brown)

1 (15 oz) can black beans, drained and rinsed

1 (15 oz) can diced tomatoes with chilies

2 tsp chili powder

1 tsp garlic powder

1 tsp ground cumin

1/2 tsp salt

1 8 oz pkg shredded Mexican cheese blend

## Directions

- Preheat oven to 350 degrees.
- Bring a large pot of water and 1 Tbsp salt to a boil, cook peppers until slightly softened about 3 minutes. Drain.
- Heat olive oil in skillet over medium heat; cook and stir onion in the hot oil until softened and transparent.
- Mix rice, black beans, tomatoes and onion in large bowl. Add seasonings, stir until mixed. Fold 1 1/2 cups shredded cheese into mixture. Spoon rice mixture into each pepper half, arrange in a baking dish. Sprinkle with remaining cheese.

- Bake in preheated oven until cheese is melted and bubbling, about 30 minutes.

# CHICKEN SALAD WITH TARRAGON

*Diabetic Friendly*

## Ingredients

1 lb boneless chicken breast

1 1/2 cups celery, chopped

2 1/2 tsp chopped fresh tarragon

1 cup chopped fresh parsley

1 cup dried cranberries

1 bunch green onions, sliced

1(8 oz) bottle fat free raspberry vinaigrette dressing

spring mix greens

strawberries, optional

## Directions

- Cook chicken breast in covered skillet with small amount of water until tender. Cool and shred
- In a large bowl, mix the shredded chicken, celery, tarragon, parsley, dried cranberries, onion and salad dressing.
- Refrigerate at least 1 hour or overnight.
- To serve, line a large bowl with spring mix and place chicken salad in center. Garnish with fresh strawberries, if desired.

# CHICKEN FRIED RICE

## Ingredients

- 1 Tbsp olive oil
- 4 green onions, green & white separated, chopped
- 1 Tbsp fresh ginger, grated
- 2 cloves garlic, minced
- 1 med yellow squash, diced
- 2 carrots, diced
- 2 cups bite-size broccoli florets
- 2 cups mushrooms, sliced
- 1/2 lb boneless, skinless chicken thighs or breasts, sliced thin
- 4 cups cooked brown rice
- 2 Tbsp low-sodium soy sauce
- 2 eggs, slightly beaten

## Directions

- Using a wok or large skillet, heat oil over med-high heat.
- Add onion whites, ginger, and garlic and cook for 30-45 seconds.
- Add squash, carrots, broccoli and mushrooms and cook 4-5 minutes using a spatula to stir vegetables.
- Add chicken and continue cooking for 2-3 minutes until meat is no longer pink.
- Stir in rice and soy sauce and cook another 5 minutes, allowing rice to get crispy on bottom.
- Make a hole in the middle and quickly scramble eggs until light and fluffy.
- Stir eggs into rest of ingredients. Garnish with green onion tops.

# STUFFED AUBERGINES (EGGPLANT)

## Ingredients

3-4 medium-sized eggplants

1 lb ground pork or turkey

2-3 ripe tomatoes, diced

2 onions, finely diced

1/4 cup olive oil

1 bay leaf

1 clove garlic, minced

salt and pepper

olive oil for frying (note: eggplant absorbes oil)

Parmesan cheese, grated

## Directions

- Preheat oven to 350 degrees.
- Lightly sauté onions in olive oil.
- Add ground meat and cook for 10 minutes stirring constantly.
- Add tomatoes, garlic, bay leaf, salt and pepper and a small amount of water and simmer for 1 hour.
- In the meantime, wash, peel and slice eggplant lengthwise into 1/4 inch slices. Place eggplant slices in salted water for about an hour.
- Drain eggplant slices and fry in hot oil. Layer slices in casserole dish with meat mixture.
- Cover with thick Béchamel sauce.
- Sprinkle with Parmesan cheese and bake for about 25 minutes.

## Béchamel Sauce

### Ingredients

1 cup flour

3/4 cup olive oil

continued >>

1 quart fat free milk, warmed

3 eggs, beaten

5 oz Parmesan cheese, grated

salt and pepper, to taste

pinch of nutmeg

## Directions

- Mix oil and flour in large sauce pan and cook over medium heat for 5 minutes.
- Add warmed milk whisking constantly with wire whip.
- Beat eggs and add to mixture. Add salt, pepper and nutmeg and cook for 5 minutes stirring constantly.
- Add grated cheese. If too thick, add small amount of milk.

## Notes

# Side Dishes

*The side dishes include a variety of starchy food combinations such as brown rice, barley, potatoes, sweet potatoes, quinoa, grits, corn and dried beans along with vegetables and some fruit.*

# PASTA PRIMAVERA

Yield: 6 (2 cup) servings

## Ingredients

1 Tbsp butter

1/2 pound asparagus, cut into one inch pieces.

1/2 pound mushrooms, sliced

1 medium summer squash, sliced

1 medium carrot, sliced

1/4 cup green onion, sliced

1/2 cup frozen peas, thawed

1 tsp basil

1/2 tsp salt

1/4 tsp pepper

dash of ground pepper

1 cup fat free milk

1 1/2 Tbsp cornstarch

1/4 cup Parmesan cheese

1/4 cup fresh parsley, chopped

8 ounce dry angel hair pasta

## Directions

- Melt butter over medium heat in a large sauté pan; add first 4 vegetables.
- Cook and stir for 3 minutes. Cover and cook an additional minute.
- Follow package directions to cook pasta.
- While pasta is cooking, add next six ingredients to vegetables.
- In a separate container, combine cold milk and cornstarch.
- Add milk mixture to vegetables, stir and bring to a boil for 1 minute.
- Toss in vegetables and combine sauce mixture with pasta, then add Parmesan cheese and parsley.

## Nutrition

Calories: 218kcal; Carbohydrate: 33g; Fiber: 3g; Protein: 11g;
Fat: 6g; Cholesterol: 14mg; Sodium: 460mg
Exchanges: 1 1/2 carbohydrate choices, 1-2 vegetable choices,
1 meat and 1 fat.

# CORN FRITTERS

## Ingredients

1 1/2 cup flour
2 tsp baking powder
1 Tbsp sugar
1 egg
1/2 cup milk
1 (15 oz) can whole kernel corn
vegetable oil for frying

## Directions

- In a bowl, whisk together dry ingredients, milk and egg.
- In a large skillet, heat oil over high heat.
- Add corn into milk and egg mixture and stir. Drop by table-spoonfuls into hot oil.
- Fry mixture for 2 minutes on each side; drain on paper towel.
- Pour syrup over the fritter or eat plain.

# QUINOA

*Quinoa is a great alternative to potatoes or rice. It is high in protein and fiber, versatile and can be enhanced with fruit, nuts, or vegetables.*

## Ingredients

1 cup quinoa

2 cups water or chicken broth

2 Tbsp lemon juice

## Directions

- Place all ingredients in a sauce pan; bring to a boil. Cover and simmer for 12-15 minutes or until liquid is absorbed.

Option: 1.
In a bowl, mix the cooked quinoa with 1/4 cup each of the diced dried apricots, cranberries and walnuts. Serve as a side dish with chicken or pork.

Option 2:
In a sauté pan, sauté the sliced fresh mushrooms, diced red onions, and add 1 tsp minced garlic into 1 Tbsp of olive oil cook until tender. Mix sauté mixture with the cooked quinoa. Serve as a side dish or use the mixture as a stuffing in bell peppers for a main dish.

# SWEET POTATO and APPLE SALAD

Yield: 12 servings (great alternative to regular potato salad)

## Ingredients

3 pounds sweet potato, peeled and diced into 1/2 inch pieces

1/2 pound celery, diced into 1/4 inch pieces

1 red onion, diced into 1/4 inch pieces

1 pound apples, peeled and diced

1 cup dried cranberries, plumped in warm water

1/2 cup pecans, coarsely chopped

2 Tbsp sesame seeds (optional)

## Dressing:

1/2 cup canola oil

1/2 cup vegetable stock thickened with 1/2 Tbsp cornstarch

juice of 2 lemons

1/4 cup apple cider vinegar

1 tsp salt

1/2 tsp pepper

1/4 cup sugar

## Directions

- Preheat oven to 375 degrees.
- Combine all dressing ingredients and emulsify in a blender.
- Place potatoes onto a large sheet pan with sides; roast potatoes for about 15 minutes or until tender.
- Combine celery, onion and apples into pan with dressing and mix gently.
- Refrigerate 2-3 hours and garnish with sesame seeds.

## Nutrition

Calories: 327kcal; Protein: 3g; Fat: 17g; Saturated Fat: 1g; Carbohydrates: 43g; Sodium: 373 mg; Fiber: 6g

# SOUTHWEST PASTA SALAD

Yield: 8 servings

## Ingredients

1 box Dreamfields brand elbows or penne pasta

1 cup cherry or grape tomatoes, halved

1 red bell pepper, cut into thin strips

1 large sweet onion, halved and thinly sliced

1 avocado, diced

1/4 cup cilantro, chopped

1 to 2 jalapeno chilies, seeded and chopped

1 cup reduced-fat mayonnaise

1 cup tomato salsa

1 Tbsp fresh lime juice

## Directions

- Cook pasta according to directions on package. Drain excess water and rinse pasta with cold water. Drain again.
- In a large serving bowl, combine pasta, tomatoes, bell pepper, onion, avocado, cilantro and jalapeno.
- For dressing, whisk together in a small bowl the mayonnaise, salsa, and lime juice.
- Combine pasta mixture and dressing in a large bowl and toss gently. Serve immediately or cover bowl and refrigerate to serve chilled.

Note: This is not the usual pasta salad. It is a mixture of flavors from cool and creamy to hot and spicy. It is great for cook-outs or pot lucks.

## Nutrition

(1/8 of recipe) Calories: 313kcal; Protein: 8g; Carbohydrates: 12g (using Dreamfields brand pasta); Fat: 14g; Saturated Fat: 2g; Cholesterol: 13mg; Sodium: 595mg; Fiber: 7g

# POTATO PANCAKES

Yield: approximately 20 pancakes

## Ingredients

5 potatoes, grated

2 onions

3 eggs

1 tsp salt

1/4 tsp pepper

Between 1/4 to 3/4 cup all-purpose flour

canola oil for frying

## Directions

- Using a sharp knife or potato peeler, peel and grate the potatoes and onions.
- Place the potatoes into a bowl of cold water so potatoes won't turn brown. When ready to prepare pancakes, drain potatoes.
- Pour potato and onion mixture into a large bowl. Add beaten eggs to the mixture. Season with salt and pepper.
- Add enough flour so that the mixture holds together.
- Pour oil into a large frying pan or a griddle over medium-high heat.
- Carefully drop 1/4 cup of the potato mixture onto pan.
- Fry for several minutes on each side until golden brown and cooked through.
- Drain pancakes on paper towels.

Serving Suggestion: Serve the pancakes with applesauce, sour cream or plain yogurt.

# DUMPLINGS

*This dumpling recipe came entirely from my mother's memory; there wasn't a written recipe. It took me many tries to get an acceptable dumpling so I could write it down. It is one of my grandchildren's favorite dishes.*

## Ingredients

whole chicken

carrots, celery, onion and garlic cloves

4 cups flour

1/2 cup powdered buttermilk

1/2 tsp baking soda

2 Tbsp shortening

1 3/4 - 2 cups chicken broth

salt and pepper, to taste

## Directions

- In a large pot, cook large fryer chicken in enough water to cover, add carrots, celery, onion and garlic cloves. Cook for approximately 1 hour or when internal tempertaure reaches 180 degrees.
- Remove vegetables from pot, allowing them to cool. Remove chicken from pot and let cool. Remove chicken meat from bones and set aside.
- In a large bowl mix together flour, powdered buttermilk and baking soda. Fold in shortening.
- Add chicken broth gradually to soften the dough.
- Knead once or twice and then roll dough to be 1/4 inch thick.
- Cut dough into 2 inch strips; drop dough strips into boiling chicken broth. Cover and cook for 10-12 minutes.
- Season with salt and black pepper to taste.
- Add chicken pieces before serving.

## Variation

- Make the dumplings following the directions above except use 1 cup of liquid.

- Add 2 or 3 egg whites to the broth.
- Mix gently until you can form the dough into a ball.
- Roll out the dough and cut into strips; add more flour as needed.

---

# GREENS and CORNBREAD
# UPSIDE DOWN CAKE

Yield: 12 servings

## Ingredients

3 bunches or 1 1/2 pounds greens (kale or swiss chard)

2 Tbsp canola or olive oil

1 medium onion

2 drops Tabasco sauce (or chopped jalapeno pepper)

1 (16 oz) can chicken broth

1/4 cup sugar or Splenda®

4 1/2 cups cornbread mix (I recommend that you make your own corn bread mix.)

2 1/2 cups buttermilk

1 clove garlic

salt and pepper

## Directions

- Preheat oven to 350 degrees.
- Wash greens thoroughly. Using a sharp paring knife, chop up greens and place in a large pot of water.
- Cover and steam until the greens are wilted; drain excess liquid.
- In a medium pan over medium heat, sauté onion, jalapeno pepper and garlic in oil.
- Add sautéed mix into the pot with the greens.
- Season greens with salt, pepper and Tabasco sauce. Pour

continued >>

chicken broth into the pot and cook approximately 15 minutes. Drain excess liquid out of the pot.

- In a medium bowl, mix together cornbread mix, adding either sugar or Splenda® and buttermilk. Do not over mix cornbread.
- Arrange greens in bottom of a greased rectangular pan lined with parchment (wax) paper.
- Pour the batter evenly over the greens and smooth out mixture with a spatula.
- Bake for 30-40 minutes, or until golden brown.
- Let stand in the pan 15 minutes before unmolding.

## Nutrition

Calories: 252kcal; Protein: 9g; Fat: 5g; Saturated Fat: 0g; Cholesterol: 2mg; Carbohydrate: 47g (varies depending on the corn bread mix used to prepare meal); Sodium: 643mg; Fiber: 4g

# Notes

# Vegetables

*My husband, Sam, grows a multitude of vegetables in his garden and during the summer we always have them available. I am able to freeze enough vegetables to last through the winter months. His garden also produces enough for friends and neighbors to enjoy. I find myself creating new and different ways to prepare vegetables because of the great abundance. Many of the recipes included in this book are ones that I have created and are diabetic friendly.*

# Author's note on vegetables

**O**ne of my career experiences was managing a diabetes self-management program where I learned a lot about people's attitudes and eating habits. One realization was that many who participated in the program were challenged to include vegetables in adequate amounts in their daily eating plan.

Some people never learned to eat vegetables for a variety of reasons. Families may not have included vegetables as part of their meals either because they did not know how to cook them to be palatable or did not know how they should taste. Also, children don't observe their parents enjoying vegetables therefore they do not have a role model for consuming them. My grandchildren enjoy all kinds of vegetables and are willing to try something new. They often have helped when I am doing cooking demonstrations which allows them to learn different techniques.

Vegetables are an important addition to meals because they provide vitamins, minerals, and fiber. The more colorful they are the more nutrient dense, packing a big punch in small amounts.

Some people live in food deserts, where access to fresh produce is limited or nonexistent; however, fast food restaurants are plentiful and they generally don't promote vegetables and fruit. The current trend toward community gardens and farmers markets has raised awareness and increased availability of fresh produce in food deserts. The challenge is how to cook and make them appetizing even if they are available.

Many of the recipes that I have included in this book are diabetic friendly and have the nutrient analysis for ease in planning what to eat.

# GRILLED VEGETABLES

*This is a family favorite during the summer outdoor grilling season.*
*These vegetables are a wonderful addition to the meal.*

## Ingredients

red, yellow, orange and green peppers, cut in half with stems and
pulp removed

eggplant, peeled and sliced (soaked in salt water before cooking),

large red onions, peeled and sliced about 1/2 inch thick

corn on the cob (do not shuck)

olive oil

kosher salt and pepper to taste

## Directions

- Brush the vegetables all over with olive oil.
- Sprinkle salt and pepper lightly over the vegetables.
- Cook on an outside grill pan until desired doneness, turning as
  needed. Be careful not to burn.

Note: Any variety of vegetable can be grilled. Summer squash,
zucchini, asparagus, sweet potatoes, white potatoes, carrots
and cauliflower are some of my favorites. These same vegetables can be roasted in the oven if you are not able to grill
outside. Try a variety of herbs to season the vegetables such
as rosemary, garlic, or basil.

# ROASTED BEETS

## Ingredients

4 or 5 beets (pink, yellow, and red with stems and leaves)

olive oil

kosher salt

balsamic vinegar

## Directions

- Preheat oven to 350 degrees.
- Wash beets and trim stems to approximately 1/2 inch.
- Rub beets with olive oil and sprinkle with kosher salt.
- Place beets into a roasting pan and cover with aluminum foil.
- Bake for approximately 1 hour. Beets are done when a knife can easily be inserted.
- Let the beets cool, then peel. The peel will slide off easily.
- Slice beets. Serve warm or place them in refrigerator to chill.

Note: I especially like to serve beets with balsamic vinegar.

# SOUTHERN STYLE BLACK-EYED PEAS

Yield: 4 (1 cup) servings

## Ingredients

1 lb dried black-eyed peas

1 medium onion, diced

1 medium carrot, thinly sliced

1 serrano or jalapeno pepper, seeded and thinly sliced (optional)

4 oz lean smoke-flavored ham, with visible fat removed, diced

water, enough to cover peas

## Directions

Crock-pot directions:
- Rinse peas under cold running water.
- Place all ingredients into crock pot; add enough water to cover peas.
- Cook on low setting for 8 to 10 hours, or until peas are tender.

Stove-top directions:
- Rinse peas under cold running water.
- Place all ingredients into a large saucepan or Dutch oven.
- Add enough water to cover the peas.
- Bring to a boil over medium high heat; skim off foam on top.
- Reduce heat to medium-low. Cover and simmer for 2 hours, or until peas are tender.

## Nutrition

Calories: 148kcal; Fat: 3g; Protein 5.2g; Carbohydrates 33.5g

# STEWED TOMATOES and OKRA

Yield: 8 Servings

## Ingredients

8 large fresh tomatoes (If fresh tomatoes are unavailable,
use 1 (28 oz) can tomatoes.)

2 tsp reduced-fat margarine or olive oil

2 medium onions, chopped

1 green bell pepper, seeded and chopped

fresh or frozen okra (16 oz) chopped

1 cup frozen corn

2 tsp sugar

1/2 cup dried breadcrumbs

## Directions

- Plunge the tomatoes into a pot of boiling water for 1 minute to make them easier to peel.
- Cool tomatoes slightly, then peel and chop.
- Heat margarine or oil in a large skillet and sauté the tomatoes, onions, and bell pepper.
- Add okra, corn, and sugar and simmer on low heat for 25 minutes.
- To thicken the mixture, add breadcrumbs and stir well.

## Nutrition

Calories: 128kcal; Fat: 2g; Saturated Fat: 0g; Cholesterol: 0mg;
Sodium: 85mg; Protein: 5g; Carbohydrate: 26g; Dietary Fiber: 5g

# CREAMY MASHED CAULIFLOWER

*My husband thought these were mashed potatoes the first time I served them!*

Yield: 8 servings

## Ingredients

> 1 large head cauliflower, cut into pieces
>
> 2 cloves garlic
>
> 1/4-1/2 cup mayonnaise

## Directions

- In a medium saucepan over medium high heat, bring water and cauliflower to a boil.
- Add garlic cloves and cook on medium heat for 15 minutes or until tender.
- Drain off liquid from pan.
- Process cauliflower, garlic and mayonnaise in a food processor until mixture is creamy.
- Season to taste with pepper and dash of salt, if desired.

Note: A bay leaf and or whole allspice may be added to the water to cook the cauliflower for added flavor. Remove when the cauliflower is tender.

## Nutrition

> Calories: 108 kcal; Protein: 2g; Fat: 10g; Saturated Fat: 1g; Cholesterol: 4mg; Sodium: 211mg; Fiber: 3g.

# FIVE VEGGIE STIR FRY

Yield: 4 (2 cup) servings  (serving = one cup rice, one cup veggies)

## Ingredients

2 Tbsp cornstarch

2 Tbsp sugar

1/2 tsp ground ginger or fresh grated

1 cup orange juice

1/4 cup reduced-sodium soy sauce

2 garlic cloves, minced

2 large carrots, sliced

2 cups broccoli florets

2 cups cauliflower, cut into bite-sized pieces

4 tsp olive or canola oil, divided

1 cup fresh mushrooms, quartered

1 cup fresh or frozen snow peas

4 cups hot cooked brown rice

## Directions

- In a small bowl combine cornstarch, sugar and ginger.
- Stir in orange juice, soy sauce and garlic; mix well until blended. Set aside in a nonstick skillet or wok.
- Stir-fry carrots, broccoli and cauliflower in 3 teaspoons of oil for 4-5 minutes.
- Add in mushrooms, peas and remaining 1 teaspoon oil; stir-fry vegetables for 3 minutes. Stir in orange juice mixture and bring to a boil over medium high heat. Stir vegetables and liquid mixture and cook until thickened.
- Serve immediately over rice.

## Nutrition

Calories: 382kcal; Fat: 5g; Cholesterol: 0g; Sodium: 648mg; Carbohydrate: 74g; Fiber: 3g; Protein: 9g

*Nutrition for rice:* Calories 218kcal; Carbohydrate 45.8; Protein 4.5

# SUMMER SQUASH

## Ingredients

3 or 5 medium yellow summer squash, washed and sliced into
1/4 inch thick slices

1 large onion, peeled and sliced thin

2 Tbsp olive oil

sugar or Splenda® (to taste)

salt and pepper (to taste)

## Directions

- Wash squash and slice into 1/4 inch thick slices.
- Peel onion and slice into thin slices.
- Heat olive oil in a large skillet; add vegetables.
- Cover the vegetables and cook until tender, stirring occasionally to prevent sticking.
- Season to taste with salt, pepper and sugar or sweetener.

Note: Squash contains water and by cooking the squash covered it will generate enough liquid.

Options: Steam the squash and onions. Add seasonings, and mix with 2 eggs beaten or 1/2 cup egg whites. Pour into a greased casserole dish and dot with buttered bread cubes. Bake 350 degrees for about 20 minutes.

---

# STEAMED CABBAGE

## Ingredients

1 large head green cabbage, washed and cut into 1/2 inch shreds

1 medium bell pepper (orange or red for color), seeded and sliced

1 Tbsp. salad oil

1 (14 oz) can chicken broth

## Directions

- Place oil into a large skillet or pot with lid.
- Add cabbage. Add peppers on top of cabbage and pour chicken broth over cabbage and peppers.
- Bring to a boil over medium high heat, reduce heat to low and simmer for approximately 10-15 minutes.
- Season with salt and pepper.

# ORANGE CARROTS

## Ingredients

2 pounds carrots, peeled and cut in strips

2 Tbsp reduced fat margarine

1 medium Vidalia onion, thinly sliced

1 cup orange juice

1 (8 oz) can Mandarin oranges

dash of salt

## Directions

- Preheat oven to 350 degrees.
- Place carrots, onions, mandarin oranges and margarine into a baking dish.
- Add orange juice and salt to baking dish and cover tightly.
- Bake 30 to 45 minutes or until carrots can be easliy pierced with a fork.

## Nutrition

Calories: 101kcal; Fat: 1g; Carbohydrate: 22g; Sodium:177mg

# MIXED GREENS

## Ingredients

4 bunches of greens, wash, remove stems and cut into small pieces. (mustard, collards, kale)

2 Tbsp olive or salad oil

2-3 small peppers, chopped (select peppers based on desired degree of hotness)

1 large onion chopped

1-2 cloves garlic (minced)

1 (28 oz) can beef, chicken or vegetable broth

## Directions

- Place greens in a large pot with broth. Cook on medium high heat and bring to a boil.
- Sauté onions, peppers and garlic in oil until tender.
- Add sauté mixture to greens, cover and continue cooking for approximately 30 minutes or until desired doneness.
- Season with salt and pepper to taste.

# BROCCOLI WITH CARMALIZED SHALLOTS

Yield: 4 servings

## Ingredients

2 Tbsp walnut pieces

1 1/2 tsp extra virgin olive oil

1 cup shallots (4-5 large) sliced

1 bunch broccoli (1 1/2 lb) cut into florets

salt and pepper to taste

## Directions

- Preheat oven to 450 degrees.
- Place walnuts in a pie plate and toast in the oven for 5 minutes or until fragrant. Transfer toasted walnuts into a bowl.
- Heat oil in a large nonstick skillet over medium-low heat.
- Add shallots and cook for 10 minutes or until deep golden brown. (Add a tablespoon or two of water to the skillet if it gets too dry.)
- Cook broccoli in boiling salted water for 3-5 minutes or until tender. Drain broccoli and add it to the shallots; mix well.
- Season to taste.
- Transfer broccoli and shallots to a serving bowl and sprinkle with toasted walnuts.

# GEORGIA CAVIAR

*Recipe from "Cooking Healthy Across America" American Dietetic Association*

Yield: 12 (1/3 cup) servings

## Ingredients

2 (15 oz) cans black-eyed peas, drained and rinsed

1 1/2 cups low-fat vinaigrette dressing

1 (7 oz) jar roasted red peppers, diced

1 small onion, diced (about 3/4 cup)

1/4 cup diced jalapenos, seeds and ribs removed

1/2 cup black olives, sliced

1/2 cup mushrooms, sliced

1 clove garlic, minced

1/4 to 1/2 tsp black pepper

2 (10 oz) bags mixed, or mesclun greens

## Directions

- Place all the ingredients except the greens into a bowl and mix well.
- Serve the caviar over a bed of greens.

## Nutrition

Calories: 220kcal; Fat: 15g; Saturated Fat: 2g; Cholesterol: 0mg; Sodium: 520mg; Carbohydrate: 14g; Dietary Fiber: 5g; Protein: 5g

## Variation

Dried peas

- Soak 1/2 pound of dried black-eyed peas in 1 quart of water in a large bowl overnight.
- Drain the peas and combine them in a large saucepan with 1 quart of chicken or vegetable broth.
- Bring to a boil over medium high heat.
- Reduce heat to low; cover and simmer for 30 to 40 minutes or until tender.

Cook's Tip:
Always wear protective gloves when handling jalapenos or other hot peppers. Wash the cutting surface well after each use or use a disposable cutting surface.

Note: This is good over cooked greens or salad greens.

# GREEN BEANS with WALNUTS

Yield: 12 servings

## Ingredients

1 cup walnuts, chopped

4 pounds green beans, washed and trimmed

3 Tbsp butter

3 red peppers, diced 1/4 inch

1/4 cup parsley, chopped

3/4 tsp salt

1/4 tsp pepper

4 Tbsp walnut oil

## Directions

- Preheat oven to 350 degrees.
- Roast walnuts in a preheated oven for 5-10 minutes.
- Cook green beans in boiling salted water until tender; drain.
- Melt butter in a sauté pan and saute the red peppers until tender.
- Add beans and toss.
- Add walnuts and parsley and toss.
- Finish with salt, pepper and walnut oil.

# HERBED SPAGHETTI SQUASH

Yield: 4-6 (1/2 cup) servings

## Ingredients

1 spaghetti squash (about 2 1/4 lbs)

1 Tbsp butter

1 Tbsp olive oil

1 Tbsp each: chopped parsley, basil, chives (preferably fresh)

1/4 tsp black pepper

## Directions

- Using a fork or sharp knife, make slits in spaghetti squash to vent.
- Place squash into a microwave and cook until tender, testing with a fork. Allow to cool slightly.
- Cut squash in half; remove seeds and discard.
- Using a fork, gently pull strands of squash away from peel and place in a mixing bowl.
- Heat butter and oil in a large skillet. Add spaghetti squash, herbs and pepper. Toss gently but thoroughly to heat and combine. Serve immediately or cover and keep warm until ready to serve.

## Nutrition

Calories 150; Total Fat 7g; Saturated Fat 2.5g; Trans Fat 0g; Colesterol 10mg; Sodium 490mg; Total Carbohydrates 13g; Sugars 5g; Protein 1g

# BRAISED CHARD
# with GINGER and COCONUT

*Chard is lightly braised in a broth of coconut milk, fresh ginger and a hint of red pepper flakes.*

Yield: 4 servings

## Ingredients

1 large bunch green chard

1 Tbsp olive oil

1/2 medium sweet onion, thinly sliced

2 cloves garlic, thinly sliced

1 Tbsp grated fresh ginger

continued >>

1/4 cup vegetable broth

1/4 cup coconut milk

1/2 tsp kosher salt

1/4 tsp black pepper

pinch of red pepper flakes

## Directions

- Tear chard into pieces; set aside. Heat olive oil in large sauté pan over medium high heat.
- Sauté onions for 3 minutes or until they begin to brown, add garlic and sauté 1 minute
- Add chard and remaining ingredients to pan. Cover and cook over low heat for 8-10 minutes.
- Serve immediately.

# MIXED GREENS AND CABBAGE

Yeild: 8 (1/2 cup) servings

## Ingredients

1 tsp olive oil

1/2 medium onion, thinly sliced

2 cups fat-free, low-sodium chicken broth

2 Tbsp imitation bacon bits

1 tsp garlic powder

1 tsp celery seeds

1/4 tsp pepper

1/4 tsp crushed red pepper flakes

4 ounces fresh collard greens

4 ounces fresh kale

8 ounces green cabbage

## Directions

- In a large saucepan, heat oil over medium heat, swirling to coat the bottom. Cook onion for 2 to 3 minutes, or until tender-crisp, stirring occasionally.
- Stir in broth, bacon bits, garlic powder, celery seeds, pepper, and red pepper flakes. Increase heat and continue to simmer, covered, for 4 to 5 minutes allowing flavors to blend.
- Meanwhile, trim stems from collard greens and kale; discard stems. Core cabbage; discard core. Coarsely chop greens and cabbage and stir into broth mixture. Adjust heat and simmer covered, for 35 to 45 minutes, stirring occasionally, or until greens and cabbage are tender. Ladle the greens and pot likker (cooking liquid) into bowls.

## Nutrition

Per 1/2 cup Serving:

Calories 36; Carbohydrates 5g; Total Fat 1g; Dietary Fiber 2g;

Saturated Fat 0g; Protein 2g; Cholesterol 0mg; Sodium 61mg;

Polyunsaturated Fat 0g; Sugars 2g; Monounsaturated Fat 0.5g

Dietary Exchanges: 1 vegetable

# Notes

# Desserts

*My mother always made cakes for the holidays. She made yellow cake with chocolate frosting, white cake with coconut filling and frosting, pound cake and marble cake. These cakes were light with a fine grain texture and we always looked forward to having them. She also made grape wine from the grapes that grew wild (we called them 'possum grapes) in the fall of the year. We only had this wine at Christmas time.*

*My holiday baking is mainly cookies because the cakes made at high altitude were not the same texture as the southern cakes I was used to. My learning curve for making cakes at high altitude was quite steep. I could not duplicate my mother's cakes so I focused on baking cookies. I often include my grandchildren in the cookie making process, allowing them to make and decorate. Now I enjoy making cookies to give during the holidays.*

# OATMEAL SCOTCHIES

*Cheryl Pegues*

Yield: approximately 4 dozen

## Ingredients

1 cup (2 sticks) butter, softened

3/4 cup granulated sugar

3/4 cup firmly packed brown sugar

2 eggs

1 tsp vanilla

1 1/4 cups all-purpose flour

1 tsp baking soda

1/2 teaspoon salt (optional)

3 cups Quaker oats (old fashioned, uncooked)

1 1/4 cups butterscotch pieces

1 1/2 cups chopped walnuts

1 cup Baker's sweetened flaked coconut

## Directions

- Preheat oven to 375 degrees.
- Beat the butter, sugars, eggs and vanilla until creamy.
- Combine in a separate bowl flour, baking soda and salt. Add this to butter and sugar mixture and mix well.
- Stir in oats, butterscotch pieces, nuts and coconut; mix well.
- Drop dough by level tablespoonfuls onto ungreased cookie sheets. (You can also line cookie sheet with parchment paper and bake ungreased.)
- Bake for 8-9 minutes for a chewy cookie or bake for 10-12 minutes for a crisp cookie.
- Cool for 2 minutes on cookie sheets. Remove to wire rack.
- Let cookies cool completely. Store in a air-tight container.

# JUMBO RAISIN COOKIES

## Ingredients

4 cups flour

1 tsp baking powder

1/2 tsp salt

1 1/4 tsp cinnamon

1/4 tsp allspice

1/4 tsp nutmeg

2 cups raisins

1 cup water

1 cup shortening

2 cups sugar

3 eggs

1 tsp vanilla

1 cup chopped nuts

## Directions

- Preheat oven to 375 degrees.
- Sift together the first 6 ingredients.
- in a saucepan, bring to boil the raisins in 1 cup water; boil for 5 minutes. Set aside and let cool.
- Cream together shortening and sugar. Add eggs, one at a time, beating egg well after each addition. Add vanilla, nuts and cooled raisin mixture.
- Drop dough by using a teaspoon on greased cookie sheet.
- Bake at for 12-15 minutes.

# ULTIMATE BUTTER COOKIES

*Recipe from the Western Dairy Association. Great for holidays!*

## Ingredients

1 cup unsalted butter, softened

1/2 cup sugar

1/2 tsp salt

1 large egg yolk

2 1/4 cups all-purpose flour

red and green decorator sugar

## Directions

- Preheat oven to 350 degrees.
- Using an electric mixer, cream together butter with sugar, salt and egg yolk until smooth.
- Gradually beat in flour.
- Wrap dough in plastic wrap and refrigerate 1 hour.
- Dough can be refrigerated up to 2 days.

*During this time, flavors blend and develop, bringing out the butter flavor of the dough.*

- Roll out the dough on a lightly floured surface to 1/8 inch thickness.
- Cut into desired shapes using holiday cookie cutters.
- Place on lightly greased cookie sheets.
- Sprinkle dough with decorator sugar.
- Bake for 12-15 minutes.

Note: Recipe tested at high altitude. This is an outstanding basic butter cookie recipe.

# GINGER SNAPS

*A family favorite*

Yield: 5 dozen

## Ingredients

3/4 cup butter

1 cup brown sugar

1/4 cup molasses

1 egg

2 1/4 cups all-purpose flour

2 tsp baking soda

1/2 tsp salt

1 tsp ginger

1 tsp cinnamon

1/4 tsp cloves

## Directions

- Preheat oven to 375 degrees.
- Cream together butter, sugar, and molasses.
- Add the egg and beat until smooth.
- Sift flour, soda, and spices together and add to molasses mixture, stirring to combine thoroughly.
- Form dough into small balls.
- Roll dough balls in granulated sugar and place on a greased cookie sheet.
- Bake for 12 minutes.

# BUTTERSCOTCH ICE BOX COOKIES

## Ingredients

1 cup butter

2 cups brown sugar

pinch of salt

2 eggs beaten

2 tsp vanilla

3 cups all-purpose flour

1 tsp baking soda

1 cup nuts, chopped

## Directions

- Preheat oven to 400 degrees.
- Cream together the butter, sugar and salt; add in eggs and vanilla. Beat mixture well.
- Sift flour and soda and add this to butter and sugar mixture.
- Add nuts and more flour, if needed.
- Shape dough into a long roll and wrap in waxed paper.
- Chill in refrigerator overnight.
- Slice chilled dough roll into thin slices.
- Bake for 10 minutes.

# OATMEAL COOKIES

## Ingredients

1 1/4 cups flour

1 tsp baking soda

1 cup butter

1/4 cup granulated sugar

3/4 cup brown sugar

3 ounce package instant vanilla pudding

2 eggs

3 1/2 cups oatmeal

1 cup raisins or dried cranberries (optional)

## Directions

- Preheat oven to 375 degrees.
- Sift together flour and soda; set aside.
- Cream together butter and sugars. Add eggs and vanilla pudding; mix well.
- Stir in flour and oatmeal a little at a time.
- Add raisins. Cookie dough will become stiff.
- Drop the dough by rounded tablespoonfuls onto an ungreased cookie sheet.
- Bake for 10 minutes or until done.

# CHOCOLATE CHIP COOKIES

## Ingredients

2 1/4 cups flour

1 tsp baking soda

1 cup butter

1/4 cup granulated sugar

3/4 cup brown sugar

1 tsp vanilla

1 egg

1 3 (oz) package instant pudding (chocolate or flavor of choice)

1 (10 oz) package chocolate chips

1 cup chopped nuts

## Directions

- Preheat oven to 375 degrees.
- Sift together flour and baking soda.
- Cream together well butter, sugars and vanilla.
- Add in eggs, pudding and flour; mix well.
- Stir in chocolate chips and nuts. Batter will become stiff.
- Drop dough by rounded tablespoonfuls on an ungreased cookie sheet.
- Bake for 10 minutes or until done.

# MATTIE'S 7-UP POUND CAKE

## Ingredients

- 1 cup butter
- 1/2 cup oil
- 3 cups sugar
- 5 eggs
- 3 cups flour
- 1 cup 7-Up (not diet)
- 1 tsp lemon extract
- 1/2 tsp almond extract

## Directions

- Preheat oven to 350 degrees.
- Prepare a bundt cake pan, greased and floured
- Cream together butter, oil and sugar.
- Add in eggs one at a time.
- Mix in flour alternating with 7 up and flavorings.
- Bake in prepared pan for 1 hour and 15 minutes.

## High Altitude Adjustments

- Reduce sugar to 2 1/2 cups.
- Increase number of eggs to 6.
- Use all-purpose flour and increase by 1/4 cup.
- Sift dry ingredients together after measuring flour.
- Increase 7-up by 2 tbsp.
- Bake at 325 degrees.

# RED VELVET CAKE

*Mattie Sparks*

## Ingredients

2 1/2 cups flour, sifted

1 1/2 cups sugar

1 tsp baking soda

1 tsp cocoa

1 cup buttermilk

1 1/2 cups oil

1 tsp vinegar

2 eggs

1 bottle red food coloring

1 tsp vanilla

## Directions

- Preheat oven to 350 degrees.
- Sift together all dry ingredients.
- Add other ingredients in order given and beat thoroughly.
- Bake in layer pans that have been lightly greased and floured for 30-40 minutes.

## Frosting

1 stick butter
1 8oz package cream cheese
1 box powdered sugar
1 cup chopped nuts
1/2 tsp vanilla

- Mix together thoroughly and spread in between layers and sides of cake.

# BETTYE'S PUMPKIN BREAD

## Ingredients

3 cups flour

juice of one orange

1 tsp cinnamon*

1 tsp orange zest

1 tsp nutmeg*

chopped nuts, optional

1 tsp baking powder

1/2 tsp baking soda

1/2 tsp salt

1 tsp allspice*

1 tsp ground cloves*

3 cups sugar

1 cup vegetable oil

3 eggs beaten

1 cup pumpkin

* 4 tsp pumpkin pie spice may be substituted for cinnamon, nutmeg, allspice and cloves.

## Directions

- Preheat oven to 350 degrees.
- Sift together first 8 dry ingredients, except nuts, and set aside.
- In a large mixing bowl, mix together sugar and oil.
- Add in eggs and pumpkin; mix well.
- Fold in dry ingredients alternately with orange juice.
- Add in orange zest and nuts, if desired.
- Pour into two greased and floured loaf pans.
- Bake for 45-55 minutes; test for doneness with a toothpick.

Hint: Bread baked in a 13-ounce coffee can makes a nicely designed bread for holiday giving.

# THE WESTERNER POUND CAKE

## Ingredients

3 sticks (3/4 lb) butter or margarine, room temperature

1 (lb) carton Imperial 10X Powdered Sugar

1 (lb) Imperial 10X Powdered Sugar carton full of sifted flour

6 eggs, room temperature

1 tsp lemon juice

1 Tbsp vanilla extract

## Directions

- Preheat oven to 325 degrees.
- With an electric mixer, cream together butter and sugar until fluffy.
- Add eggs, one at a time, beat well after each addition.
- Sift flour 3 times and add gradually to batter.
- Add lemon juice and vanilla; mix well. Bake in a 10" greased and floured tube pan for 1 1/2 hours.
- Cool for 4 minutes and then invert the pan.

Note: Delicious served plain with Imperial 10X Powdered Sugar sprinkled lightly into the ridges on top of the cake. Can top with ice cream, fruit, whipped cream or dessert sauce.

# ETHEL'S PECAN PIE

Yield: 16 servings

## Ingredients

1 cup sugar

1/2 cup of corn syrup (Karo)

1/4 cup melted butter

3 large eggs

1 1/2 cups pecan halves

1 unbaked 9" pie shell

## Directions:

- Preheat oven to 400 degrees.
- Mix together sugar, syrup and butter.
- Beat in eggs and add pecans to mixture.
- Pour into pie shell.
- Bake for 10 minutes at 400 degrees; lower temperature to 350 degrees and bake 35-40 minutes longer.

Note: This recipe makes 16 tarts, from purchased frozen tart shells in aluminum pans. Cooking time is reduced. Tarts are done when a toothpick inserted into the center comes out clean.

# THEASTER'S 7 UP POUND CAKE

## Ingredients

1 cup butter, softened

1/2 cup Crisco

2 1/2 cups sugar

3 cups cake flour

7 eggs

1 tsp vanilla extract

1 tsp lemon extract

5 ounces 7-Up soda

## Directions

- Preheat the oven to 300 degrees.
- Prepare a tube pan (grease and flour).
- Cream together the butter, Crisco and sugar.
- Add eggs one at a time; add vanilla and lemon extract.
- Add flour a little at a time.
- Beat ingredients well, ending with flour.
- Add in 7-Up, fold into mixture.
- Pour into prepared (greased and floured) tube pan and bake for 1 hour or until done (toothpick test).

Note: This cake is delicious with ice cream or fresh fruit.
Freezes well.

# VANILLA ICE CREAM

*Charmetra Roberts*

## Ingredients

4 12 (oz) cans evaporated milk

4 eggs

2 cups sugar

4 cups whole milk

1 tsp vanilla extract

1 tsp lemon extract

dash salt

## Directions

- Mix whole milk, sugar and eggs in pot and combine well.
- Cook over medium heat and bring to boil, stirring constantly.
- Add a dash of salt, evaporated milk and extracts.
- Pour into a gallon-size ice cream maker.
- Add ice and rock salt alternately around freezer until full.
- Plug in and freeze according to freezer directions or until turning becomes slow.
- Wipe and remove lid carefully to avoid getting salt into ice cream.

# PECAN-BOURBON BUNDT CAKE

*From my granddaughter, Yaa*

## Ingredients

Nut filling

> Mix ingredients below together and set aside.
>
> 1 cup pecans toasted and chopped fine
>
> 1/2 cup packed brown sugar
>
> 2 Tbsp unsalted butter, melted and cooled

Cake

> 1 1/4 cup unsalted butter
>
> 3 cups all-purpose flour
>
> 1/2 tsp salt
>
> 1 tsp baking powder
>
> 1/2 tsp baking soda
>
> 1/2 cup buttermilk, room temperature
>
> 1/4 cup light molasses
>
> 1/4 cup bourbon
>
> 1 Tbsp vanilla
>
> 1 3/4 cups granulated sugar
>
> 3 eggs, room temperature
>
> 1 large egg yolk, room temperature

Bourbon Glaze

> 1 3/4 cups powdered sugar
>
> 2 Tbsp bourbon
>
> 1 Tbsp light molasses
>
> 1 Tbsp water
>
> Pinch of salt

## Directions

- Preheat oven to 350 degrees.
- Butter and flour a 12 cup bundt pan.

- Sift flour, salt, baking powder and baking soda together in a medium bowl; set aside.
- In a small bowl, whisk buttermilk, molasses, bourbon and vanilla together; set aside.
- In a large bowl beat butter and sugar together on medium speed for 3–6 minutes until light and fluffy.
- Beat in eggs and egg yolk one at a time, for about 1 minute.
- Reduce mixer speed to low and beat in one 1/3 of flour mixture, followed by one half of buttermilk mixture.
- Beat in remaining flour and buttermilk mixture until just incorporated.
- Using a spatula, scrape half of batter into prepared pan.
- Smooth top; sprinkle evenly with nut filling.
- Scrape remaining batter over nuts and smooth the top.
- Bake for 50-60 minutes until skewer inserted into center comes out clean. Rotate pan halfway through baking.
- Let cake cool in pan for 10 minutes and then flip out on to a wire rack.
- Let cake cool completely, about 2 hours.

Glaze

- Whisk all glaze ingredients together until smooth.
- Let mixture sit for about 25 minutes until thickened.
- Drizzle bourbon glaze over top and sides of cake.
- Let glaze set for 25 minutes before serving.

Note: Myles and Yaa Shanti are my two grandchildren who enjoy cooking and being creative.

# SWEET POTATO PIE

*This recipe was created for the diabetes class.*

Yield: 10 servings
Prep Time: 20 minutes

## Ingredients

3 large cooked sweet potatoes, peeled and mashed

3/4 cup Splenda®

1/2 cup egg substitute

2 tsp vanilla

1 tsp lemon-flavored extract

1 Tbsp butter-flavored extract

1 tsp nutmeg

1 tsp lemon juice

1 1/2 cup evaporated (fat free) milk

1 (9 inch) pie shell

## Directions

- Pre heat oven to 350 degrees.
- Mix all ingredients together and beat until smooth.
- Pour into pie shell and bake for 40 minutes.

## Nutrition

Calories: 270 kcal; Calories from Fat: 39 kcal; Total Fat: 4g;
Saturated Fat: 1g; Cholesterol: 1mg; Sodium: 159mg;
Carbohydrate: 52g; Fiber: 3g; Sugar: 31g; Protein: 7g
Exchanges: 3 1/2 Carbohydrate, 1/2 Fat

# RHUBARB CHERRY CRISP

Yield: 6 servings

## Ingredients

Fruit filling

> 5 cups rhubarb diced in 1/2 pieces
>
> 1 (16 oz) can red sour pitted cherries
>
> 3/4 cup granulated sugar
>
> 3 Tbsp all-purpose flour

Topping

> 1/2 cup rolled oats
>
> 1/2 cup packed brown sugar
>
> 1/4 cup all-purpose flour
>
> 1/4 tsp each cinnamon and nutmeg
>
> 1/4 cup butter
>
> 1/4 cup chopped nuts (optional)

## Directions

- Preheat oven to 375 degrees.
- Mix together all ingredients for fruit filling and place into 9 inch glass baking dish.
- For topping, mix oats, brown sugar, flour, and spices in a medium bowl.
- Cut in butter until mixture resembles coarse crumbs.
- Stir in nuts; sprinkle topping over fruit filling.
- Bake for 30-35 minutes or until fruit is tender and topping is golden brown.

## Nutrition

> Calories: 360kcal; Total Fat: 13g; Saturated Fat: 6g;
> Cholesterol: 22mg; Sodium: 92mg; Carbohydrate: 61g;
> Fiber: 4g, Protein: 4g

# LEMON MERINGUE PIE

*Charmetra Roberts*

## Ingredients

Filling:

>1 1/2 cups sugar
>
>1/3 cup corn starch
>
>1 1/2 cups water
>
>3 egg yolks, slightly beaten
>
>3 Tbsp butter
>
>1/4 cup lemon juice
>
>1 Tbsp grated lemon rind (optional)
>
>1 pie shell, baked

Meringue:

>3 egg whites
>
>1/2 tsp cream of tartar
>
>1/4 cup sugar

## Directions

Filling:

- Preheat oven to 400 degrees.
- Mix sugar and corn starch into a sauce pan.
- Gradually stir in water. Cook gently until mixture thickens.
- Stir egg yolks into hot mixture, then pour into sauce pan.
- Boil for 1 minute stirring constantly. Remove from heat and continue to stir until smooth.
- Blend in butter, lemon juice and rind.

Meringue:

- Whip 3 egg whites until frothy.
- Add 1/2 tsp cream of tartar, and 1/4 cup sugar, continue to whip until peaks form.
- Pour filling into baked pie shell, smooth and cover with meringue mixture. Bake for 5-10 minutes until lightly browned.

# WHOLE WHEAT CARROT CAKE

Yield: 16 servings

## Ingredients

2 cups packed light brown sugar
1 3/4 cups whole wheat flour
2 tsp baking soda
1 tsp salt
1 tsp ground cinnamon
1 tsp nutmeg
1/2 tsp ground cloves
1 cup canola oil
4 eggs
3 cups grated carrots, lightly packed
1 tsp vanilla
powdered sugar (optional)

## Directions:

- Preheat oven to 350 degrees.
- Prepare 8-inch square baking pan with nonstick cooking spray and floured; set aside.
- Combine brown sugar, flour, baking soda, salt, cinnamon, nutmeg and cloves in a large bowl. Mix well.
- Stir in oil until well blended.
- Add in eggs, one at a time, beating well with electric mixer after each addition.
- Stir in carrots and vanilla.
- Pour batter into prepared pan.
- Bake for 45-55 minutes or until top of cake springs back when lightly touched.
- Let cake cool for 10 minutes.
- Sprinkle with powdered sugar before serving, if desired.

Tip: Use a food processor to quickly grate the carrots for this recipe. Use a metal blade, and pulse the carrots until they are evenly grated.

## Nutrition

Per serving: 1 (2" x 2") piece

Calories: 298kcal; Total Fat: 14g; Saturated Fat: 1g;

Cholesterol: 53g; Sodium: 344g; Carbohydrate: 39g;

Dietary Fiber: 2g; Protein: 4g

---

# PINEAPPLE CAKE

## Ingredients

Cake

1 box yellow cake mix

3/4 cup oil

3 eggs

1 small can Mandarin oranges with juice

Icing

12 ounce whipped topping

1 (16 oz) can crushed pineapple drained

1-3 (oz) package coconut instant pudding

1 tsp vanilla

## Directions

- Mix cake ingredients together using package directions.
- Bake cake as directed on box.
- For icing, mix ingredients and spread on cooled cake.

# PEACH COBBLER

*This is my favorite recipe to make and share.*

## Ingredients

Crust:

> 4 cups flour
>
> 1 Tbsp sugar
>
> 1 1/2 tsp salt
>
> 1 1/2 cups vegetable shortening
>
> 1 egg, beaten
>
> 1 Tbsp vinegar
>
> 1/2 cup ice water

Filling:

> 8 cups peaches, fresh or frozen
>
> 1 3/4 cups sugar (I use half Splenda®)
>
> 1 tsp cinnamon
>
> 1/2 tsp nutmeg
>
> 1 tsp vanilla
>
> 3 Tbsp flour

## Directions

Crust:

- In a large bowl, sift together flour, sugar and salt.
- Cut shortening into flour until mixture resembles coarse crumbs.
- Mix together egg, vinegar and water; add to flour mixture. Mix enough so it holds together when formed into a ball.
- Wrap in plastic and refrigerate for at least 30 minutes, or until well chilled.
- On a lightly floured surface, roll half of dough to fit a 9"x12" rectangular pan.

Filling:

- Preheat oven to 375 degrees.
- Mix in peaches with remaining ingredients and pour into pie crust (may need to add 1/2 cup of water depending on the juici-

ness of the peaches). Add 3-4 Tbsp of butter on top.
- Cover with remaining dough and crimp edges.
- Bake at 375 degrees for 15 minutes.
- Lower the heat to 350 degrees and cook for 45 minutes to 1 hour or until golden brown.

# PINEAPPLE CARROT CAKE

## Ingredients

2 1/4 cups all-purpose flour (measure before sifting)

2 cups sugar

3 tsp baking powdor

1 tsp baking soda

1/2 tsp salt

1 1/2 cups salad oil

4 eggs

2 cups raw carrots, grated

1 cup nuts, chopped

1 cup crushed pineapple, drained

2 tsp vanilla

## Directions

- Preheat oven to 350 degrees.
- Prepare a tube pan, greased and floured.
- Sift dry ingredients together.
- Add in oil and eggs; beat well.
- Fold in grated carrots, nuts, pineapple and vanilla.
- Pour into tube pan and bake for 1 hour, or until done.
- Serve cake plain.

# SWEET POTATO PIE

*Contreda Lewis*

## Ingredients

- 1 9" Pet deep dish pie crust
- 1 3/4 cups baked and mashed sweet potatoes
- 1 tsp salt
- 1 (12 oz) can evaporated milk
- 3 eggs
- 1 cup sugar (1 1/2 cups for sweeter pie)
- 1 tsp cinnamon
- 1/2 tsp nutmeg
- 1/2 tsp ginger
- 1 Tbsp melted butter

## Directions

- Preheat oven to 425 degrees.
- Peel and mash baked potatoes and measure out 1 3/4 cup.
- Beat together all ingredients with rotary beater.
- To get rid of any strings place batter in a blender and puree until smooth.
- Measure out 2 1/2 cups of batter for 1 pie.
- Bake for 45-55 minutes or until a knife inserted in middle comes out clean. Remember, center of pie will firm as it cools.
- Watch crust carefully; it has a tendency to brown quickly.

Contreda's Note:
I normally triple this recipe which makes enough for 5 pies with 1 cup of extra batter.

# Sauces

# MATTIE'S BBQ SAUCE

## Ingredients

1 onion, diced

1 green pepper, diced

1 Tbsp olive oil

1 (12 oz) bottle chile sauce

1 (16 oz) bottle catsup

1 (5 oz) bottle hot sauce

juice of one lemon

1 Tbsp sugar

2 (6 oz) cans tomato sauce

## Directions:

- In a large sauce pan, sauté onion and pepper in olive oil until onion becomes translucent.
- Add remaining ingredients, bring to a boil and simmer for about 20 minutes.
- Adjust seasonings to taste.

# MYLES'S BBQ SAUCE

Yield: 2 cups

## Ingredients

1 cup catsup

1 tsp lemon juice

1/4 cup light soy sauce

1 tsp minced garlic

2 Tbsp Worcestershire sauce

1 Tbsp molasses

2 tsp Grey Poupon mustard

## Directions

• Mix together and simmer on low heat for 20 minutes.

# Smoothies

*Smoothies are a great choice for a quick meal. I like to drink one before going to exercise class in the morning. It can be made with a combination of low calorie, nutrient-packed fruit, vegetables and dairy products of your choice.*

# FROSTY PINE-ORANGE YOGURT SMOOTHIE

Yield: 2 servings
Serving size: 1/2 recipe
Prep Time: 5 min

## Ingredients

12 ounces orange juice
1/2 cup pineapple chunks, drained
1 1/4 cups low fat vanilla yogurt

## Directions

- Combine all ingredients into a blender or food processor.
- Blend on high speed for 2-3 minutes or until frothy;
  serve immediately.

## Nutrition

Calories: 233kcal; Fat: 2g; Saturated Fat: 1g; Cholesterol: 7mg;
Sodium: 153mg; Calcium: 30% Daily Value; Protein: 9g;
Carbohydrate: 45g

# PEACH SMOOTHIE

Yield: 2 servings
Prep time: 10 minutes

## Ingredients

1 cup frozen peaches, unsweetened
1 cup fat free plain yogurt
1 cup fat free milk or soy milk
1 Tbsp Splenda®
1 teaspoon vanilla

## Directions

- In a blender combine frozen peach slices, yogurt, milk, sweetener and vanilla. Cover and blend until smooth.
- Pour into tall glass.

## Nutrition

Calories: 218 kcal; Fat: 4g; Saturated Fat: 2g; Cholesterol: 17mg; Sodium: 101mg; Calcium: 25% Daily Value; Protein: 8g (7g dairy protein); Carbohydrate: 38g; Fiber: 3g

# PEANUT BUTTER BANANA BREAKFAST SHAKE

Yield: 1 serving
Prep Time: 5 min

## Ingredients

1 cup fat free or low fat milk

1/2 cup frozen banana slices

1 Tbsp peanut butter

1/4 tsp ground cinnamon

1/2 tsp vanilla extract

Sweet cocoa powder (optional)

## Directions

- Combine all ingredients in a blender and blend until smooth and creamy.
- Pour into a tall glass and garnish with a sprinkle of cocoa powder, if desired.

## Nutrition

Calories: 270 kcal; Total Fat: 9g; Saturated Fat: 2g; Cholesterol: 5mg; Sodium: 220mg; Calcium: 35% Daily Value; Protein: 15g; Carbohydrate: 35g; Dietary Fiber: 3g

# Index

| | | |
|---|---|---|
| Mouth-watering Oven Freid Fish | Main Dishes | 62 |
| Spaghetti Cheese Casserole | Main Dishes | 50 |
| Almond Chicken Stir-Fry | Main Dishes | 64 |
| Ara's Baked Balsamic Chicken | Main Dishes | 57 |
| Chicken Fried Rice | Main Dishes | 76 |
| Oven Fried Chicken | Main Dishes | 56 |
| Chicken Pot Pie with Biscuits | Main Dishes | 73 |
| Chicken Salad with Tarragon | Main Dishes | 75 |
| Southwest Vegetable Chili | Main Dishes | 71 |
| Enchilidas *Yolanda Anderson* | Main Dishes | 53 |
| Bacon Grilled Fish | Main Dishes | 63 |
| Mexican Style Stuffed Peppers | Main Dishes | 74 |
| Pigs' Feet | Main Dishes | 60 |
| Baked Pork Chops | Main Dishes | 68 |
| Oven or Grilled BBQ Ribs | Main Dishes | 55 |
| Slow Cooker Mexican Casserole | Main Dishes | 51 |
| Slow Cooker Pasta Fagiola | Main Dishes | 52 |
| Lemon Ginger Spring Vegetable Stir Fry | Main Dishes | 70 |
| Fish Tacos | Main Dishes | 59 |
| Texas Red *Yolando Anderson* | Main Dishes | 50 |
| Turkey Meatloaf or Meat Balls | Main Dishes | 65 |
| Turkey Lettuce Wraps | Main Dishes | 58 |
| Saucy Turkey Meatballs | Main Dishes | 68 |
| Sesame Vegetable Stir Fry | Main Dishes | 66 |
| Corn Fritters | Side Dishes | 81 |
| Southwest Pasta Salad | Side Dishes | 85 |
| Sweet Potato Apple Salad | Side Dishes | 84 |
| Dumplings | Side Dishes | 88 |
| Greens and Cornbread Upside Down Cake | Side Dishes | 89 |
| Pasta Primavera | Side Dishes | 80 |
| Potato Pancakes | Side Dishes | 87 |
| Quinoa | Side Dishes | 82 |
| Roasted Beets | Vegetables | 94 |
| Broccoli with Caramelized Shallots | Vegetables | 104 |
| Steamed Cabbage | Vegetables | 100 |
| Orange Carrots | Vegetables | 101 |
| Creamy Mashed Cauliflower | Vegetables | 98 |
| Braised Chard with Ginger and Coconut | Vegetables | 107 |